W F L

E

TWELVE JEWS DISCOVER MESSIAH

To Hilda
love Spenn 93

Twelve Jews
Discover
Messiah

BEN HOEKENDIJK

KINGSWAY PUBLICATIONS
EASTBOURNE

ISBN 0 85476 332 5

Printed in Great Britain for
KINGSWAY PUBLICATIONS LTD
Lottbridge Drove, Eastbourne, E Sussex BN23 6NT by
Clays Ltd, St. Ives plc
Typeset by J&L Composition Ltd, Filey, North Yorkshire

Contents

Foreword

Few Gentile Christians have such a deep understanding of the role of the Jew in God's plan for history as do the Dutch. The stories of how Dutch Christians gave their lives to protect Jews during the Nazi holocaust in World War II still inspire us all.

Now a Dutch writer has recorded the exciting stories of contemporary Jews who live in Israel and have met Jesus as their Messiah. In this beautifully written book he combines ancient traditions from the Old Testament with the modern movement of the Holy Spirit—and ties it all together in the most exciting nation in the world: Israel.

This is a book I wish I had written. Ben is an old friend. We have spent long hours together talking about our mutual love for the Jews—and for the land of Israel.

When I discovered he was writing a book about the experiences of Jews in Israel who have received the Messiah I felt some strong pangs of envy. But he is the right one to do it—for he knows the depth and the danger of expressing one's faith in a hostile society.

Ben grew up in Holland during the Nazi occupation. He

was the one who introduced me to the fabled Corrie ten Boom. He knows first hand the cost of standing up for what you believe when society around you is going in a different direction. Thus he approaches this subject with much sensitivity. He knows that these twelve Jews who have discovered the Messiah are laying much on the line by allowing their testimonies to go into print. But why else know him, if we won't make him known?

Jamie Buckingham
Melbourne, Florida, USA

Introduction
Appointment in Jerusalem

It was more than mere curiosity that prompted me to travel from north to south through Israel with my cassette recorder and camera. Maybe the inspiration came from my grandfather, the well-known speaker and writer C.J. Hoekendijk, who in 1920 was already preaching the establishment of the State of Israel, years before Hitler came on the scene. At that time Israel was an unimportant and uninteresting spot in the backward world of the Middle East. But my grandfather read the prophecies about the restoration of Israel, and believed them. He was ridiculed, but history proves that he was right.

Those days that I spent walking around in Jerusalem were charged with heavenly energy. There was something in the air, like the first breath of spring, full of hope and expectation. I had the feeling that God had started fitting the pieces of his jigsaw puzzle together. One of these days, when the puzzle is complete, the Messiah will come with his kingdom of peace.

What overwhelmed me was the fervour of the Messianic expectation. I sensed that I was involved in something much greater than I could comprehend.

The more testimonies I heard, the more I became impressed by the diversity to be found in these people's experiences. One came to faith in an emotional way, another responded intellectually to what he or she read in the New Testament. Some have a thoroughly Orthodox background, others not. Some come from a typical Jewish environment, others from secular surroundings.

The opinions which they voice are purely personal. No one speaks for all—only for himself. You could try to add up these twelve testimonies and then find a common denominator. There are recurring factors, such as the strong urge to investigate: the hunger for the truth, which often pushed them into false religions, radical politics or drugs. Nearly all of them criss-crossed the globe on their travels. And they knew, without anyone telling them: I have to go home now, to Israel.

Pinchas Lapide says about this versatility:

> Every Bible word can be explained in seventy different ways within Judaism. Seventy, according to the list of peoples in Genesis 10. Judaism lacks a pope who can raise his exposition to dogma and by that make the other sixty-nine out to be heresy. 'All seventy are valid for God' is a saying which was already known in Jesus' time. This also comes about through the Hebrew language which was written without vowels. Therefore one word could be read in three or four different ways.

That's why there are twelve testimonies—in accordance with the number of tribes of the children of Israel, or the number of Jesus' disciples.

Many have asked me how I found these amazing stories, and I can only say: by the Holy Spirit. On the city bus someone asked why I was looking so happy. He turned out to be a Christian and we got into a conversation about this book. He mentioned the name of a Messianic Jew, and while the bus bumped through the Jaffa street, I wrote the name on the back of the *Jerusalem Post*. And I had found another source. That's how it continued to go.

I also became more and more impressed by the unique position these Messianic Jews occupy. They are a bridge between the synagogue and the church. Jews often think that you change religion if you decide to believe in the 'Christian' Jesus. But these men and women prove the opposite. Jesus didn't take their Jewishness away, but fulfilled it.

In the first century it wasn't a question of whether or not you, as a Jew, could believe in Jesus, because Jesus' first followers were Jews. The problem was how to deal with the Gentiles who came to faith. The apostles had a meeting about that matter in Jerusalem, as we read in Acts 15, and they came to the decision that the Gentiles didn't have to be circumcised, but that God would follow his own way with them.

The church wandered away from her Jewish roots and even began to persecute her 'elder brother'. Through this stubborn anti-Semitism it was made almost impossible for the Jews to come to Jesus.

We are now 2,000 years further on in history and the voice of the Messianic Jews is beginning to be heard again. The meaning of this for Christians is that they must make room for what God is doing. After all, the Bible promises a renewal of the covenant in Jeremiah 31:31.

Jews are going to experience a resurrection from the dead as God promised in Romans 11:15; a resurrection from the dead as priests, apostles and prophets. In addition, God is going to do something that is very close to his heart: unite Jews and Christians, according to Ephesians 2:14.

This unity is not found in uniformity, but only in Yeshua, the Head. In him they meet each other and can be made one. That has now begun. I, as a Gentile believer, took the offered hand of my Jewish friends. That they are prepared to forgive us, Christians, and accept us as equals is a wonder. And I, in turn, bless them.

At every interview with 'the twelve' we prayed together first. I often had the feeling that we were standing on holy ground. That impression remained throughout the writing and publication. We received letters from Jews and Christians alike that confirmed this; they too felt the presence of God in reading the manuscript.

We received help from different sources with the writing, printing and production of this book. We thank our translators: Debbie Visser-Rayner, Yvonne Barendregt-Willis and Alida Woodson-Meester, and also the people at Kingsway.

For Christians, we have put a glossary at the back of the book. For further study I have included a list of Messianic prophecies.

Now listen to the voice of God. He wants to tell you that he loves you.

Ben Hoekendijk
Putten, Holland

I
Samuel, the Prophet

Samuel Suran (forty-five), one of the leaders of the Messianic congregation Kehilat Brit in Jerusalem, sits behind a table displaying pictures painted by his wife Pamela in the conference hall Binyanei Hauma. He has red hair, happy eyes and a laughing mouth, surrounded by a red beard which is beginning to go grey at the edges.

I look at the paintings which are hanging on the back wall of the booth. Beautiful paintings. A series of water colours on the life of Jacob appeals to me the most. You see a rugged Jacob wrestling with the angel of the Lord. Running through the paintings are thin lines, giving them the appearance of a stained glass window.

Pamela Suran is one of the best-known Messianic artists. As Sam tells his story, we're interrupted every now and then by people who want to buy a set of paintings. An American woman says, 'I so enjoy your wife's paintings, the Holy Spirit really speaks through them.' That is precisely the difference between then and now: now the Holy Spirit speaks through Pam's pictures.

Pamela studied modern art both in America and Europe,

began to paint, and exhibited at seventeen exhibitions. By 1970 she had built up her career in the secular world. Then she met Yeshua and she knew immediately how she should use her talent: to invest in and to help extend God's kingdom.

In 1980 she travelled to Israel, exhibited at the Dugit Gallery in Tel Aviv and met Samuel. They married, and Pamela began to help her husband in his ministry as an elder in the Messianic congregation and as a speaker on prophetic subjects in Europe and America.

Sam has a clear vision about future developments in Israel. He believes that the time is ripe for a great spiritual awakening, which he calls *G'eulah Sh'leimah*, the 'full and final redemption of Israel'. He expects that over the next ten years God is going to reveal himself to his Jewish people. Jews are going to accept Yeshua as Messiah. Likewise, the 'wall of partition' between Jews and Christians will be broken down more and more during these years.

God revealed himself to Sam through the psalms in a unique and sovereign way. After he'd seen a painting by Leonardo da Vinci called 'The Last Supper', he bought and read a New Testament. God showed him how Yeshua had died for him. A sign had been hung above his head on the cross on which was written, 'This is Yeshua, the King of the Jews' (Mt 27:37). That stirred Sam to the very depths of his being, and just like Sha'ul, he 'was not disobedient to the vision from heaven' (Acts 26:19).

My name used to be Stuart Suranowitz. But when I came to Israel, I changed it to Shmuel Suran. Many immigrants do that; they change their name when they come to live here. Suranowitz is a name from the diaspora; Suran is my new Israeli name.

My grandparents were Orthodox Jews from Russia and Poland. They were from the tribe of Levi, who used to serve as priests in the Temple. Because the Second Temple, along with all the family genealogies, was destroyed in the year AD 70, we can't prove this. But from generation to generation it has been passed on from father to son that they were *kohanim*, members of the tribe of Levi. My father heard it from his father, and so on.

I grew up in New York City. In my youth I didn't have any idea who Yeshua was. I grew up with the same idea that most Jews had: that Yeshua had something to do with the Gentiles, with Mary and the Pope, the Vatican and Rome, but not with us, because we were Jewish. In the 60s there was a stirring among the young people in America, a desire to search for the meaning and purpose of life. I belonged to the group of young people who went to university to investigate everything; who experimented with everything to find the meaning of it all.

Like every young Jewish boy, I followed Jewish traditions and celebrated my *Bar Mitzvah* when I was thirteen years old. That means that before God, your family and your friends, you stand up in the synagogue and recite a passage from the *Haftarah*, and read the passage from the *Torah* for that week. This calls for a year's preparation. The rabbi teaches you; you learn to read the *Torah* and to recite prayers.

On the day of my *Bar Mitzvah* the passage to be read was Ezekiel 36:16–38, which deals with the restoration of Israel:

> For I will take you out of the nations; I will gather you from all the countries and bring you back into your own land. I will sprinkle clean water on you, and you will be clean. . . . I will give you a new heart. . . . You will live in the land I gave your forefathers; you will be my people, and I will be your God.

On that day I had a deep experience of God in the synagogue. Reading this portion from the Scriptures was the climax of what I'd experienced of God so far. As I read this portion from the prophets, I felt the presence of God strongly upon me.

But strangely enough, shortly after that I turned my back on Rabbinical Judaism, and thirteen years of seeking the purpose of life followed. On the one hand I couldn't accept the Orthodox Jewish way of life, but what else was there? I wanted, therefore, to discover for myself what life had to offer me.

I loved athletics. I was a kind of sports fanatic. I played baseball, basketball and football. I can honestly say that I was a kind of hero in my high school, and was the most valuable player on the field.

After high school I went out into the world and became more and more lost. I moved further away from God. This continued until I was twenty-six years old.

During those years I studied many of the humanistic philosophies: Freud, Engels and Marx, and other important world philosophies. I became very confused by it all. I wasn't even sure any more if God existed.

Those years culminated in a crisis which led me to read the Jewish book of prayers, my *Siddur*, again. I read the prayers and psalms and these awakened something deep inside me. My Jewish soul was touched once again, so that I could believe in the God of Abraham, Isaac and Jacob.

This came from God. As I read the word, God awakened something in my Jewish soul. I could do nothing but believe in the God who had created heaven and earth. There was an inner certainty; once more I became conscious of the existence of the God of Israel. God knew exactly which way he should speak to me. He touched my Jewish heart through the reading of the word. Intuitively I knew that the truth was in this and not in the philosophies which I'd studied at university.

In my heart there was a struggle going on between light and darkness, good and evil, the truth and the lie. As I continued to read the psalms, they began to speak to me in a very personal way. I realised that King David spoke about God as if he was his Father. He seemed to have a deep personal relationship with God. That touched me. No one spoke about this with me. No one explained the gospel to me. My mind was still full of the philosophies I studied at the university and I was hopelessly at odds with myself.

In the 60s we searched for answers to questions about the meaning of life. It was the time of the Beatles, drugs and rock 'n' roll. I had come to the conclusion that there was no truth, that life had no meaning, that the best you could do was to eat, drink and be merry. Those years were like one big party for me.

Then the Jewish feast *Rosh Hashanah* came round again, the Jewish New Year, and according to tradition, it is the day on which God judges the world and humanity. On that day of all days I was arrested, because somewhere in the north of the state of New York I was cultivating a field of marijuana. I went to prison for three days. It was when I was released on probation that I began to read my *Siddur* and, as a result, had my first encounter with God. You could say that God called me to a halt to gain my attention.

I received my degree at university and took a job as a mathematics teacher in an inner-city school in upstate New York. The students came from society's underprivileged, which for me was the main reason for taking that post—I was a sort of social worker.

This was also the period of the war in Vietnam, the time when my contemporaries were protesting strongly against the war, materialism and the hypocrisy of Western society.

I taught at that school for three and a half years. During this time I read the Old Testament for myself. I had such a hunger for God that I even read the Bible between classes or during lunch breaks. The psalms in particular appealed to me.

One day, as I was sitting in my classroom, I read Psalm 40 and suddenly something happened to me. I read:

I waited patiently for the Lord; he turned to me and heard my cry. He lifted me out of the slimy pit, out of the mud and mire; he set my feet on a rock and gave me a firm place to stand. He put a new song in my mouth, a hymn of praise to our God. Many will see and fear and put their trust in the Lord. Blessed is the man who makes the Lord his trust.

When I read that, I felt a deep bond with David. His experience was my experience. He put into words my thoughts and feelings. It was as if God was speaking to me. He said: 'Shmuel, I'm lifting you out of the slimy pit. I'm going to set your feet upon a rock, and I'm going to give you a new hymn of praise to our God.'

When I came to the verse, 'Blessed is the man who makes the Lord his trust,' I didn't understand what it meant, but I was prepared to do what it said and decided to trust God. I then resigned from my job as a teacher to begin a new life. I didn't know how I was going to support myself, I just knew that I should trust God.

I went to the headmaster of my school and told him that God had revealed himself to me and that I wanted to trust him on the basis of Psalm 40, and that I was therefore handing in my resignation. He didn't understand any of it. Actually, he thought that I was out of my mind. He wasn't a believer, but even if he had been, he probably would still have thought that I'd gone mad. So I left the school.

One day the following week I was browsing around in a bookshop. There were reproductions of different paintings hanging there and one in particular caught my attention. It was the famous painting by Leonardo da Vinci, 'The Last Supper', which portrays Yeshua with his disciples celebrating the Passover.

Pesach had always been the holiest Jewish feast day for me. The whole family came together to celebrate the deliverance from slavery in Egypt. I had heard that story all my life, ever since I was a small child. But I couldn't understand why Yeshua and his disciples were celebrating

Pesach. I was surprised that Yeshua celebrated a Jewish feast. I thought that Yeshua was the God of the Gentiles, that he had something to do with the Pope and Mary and the Vatican, but not with the Jewish people. But every year around Christmas time I heard beautiful songs about Yeshua's birth and some of them moved me, especially the song 'Noël, Noël. Born is the King of Israël'.

I asked for more information and ended up at the Bible Society where I found a New Testament. The text which I turned to was Matthew 1:1 and I read, 'A record of the genealogy of Yeshua HaMashiach the son of David, the son of Abraham. . . .' I was taken completely by surprise. God began to take the veil away from my eyes and I saw that Yeshua was a Jew. He was the son of David and the son of Abraham!

And so I began to read Matthew's Gospel with great interest. I made a serious attempt to put aside all my preconceived ideas about who Yeshua was.

When I read about the miraculous birth of Yeshua and that God had instructed Joseph to give him the name 'Immanuel', which means 'God with us', I saw the connection between the Old and the New Testament. This awakened my interest even more.

I was deeply affected when I read further about the life of Yeshua and his ministry to the Jewish people—how he preached in the synagogues, and went around healing the sick, cleansing lepers and raising the dead. I was moved by his compassion to people in need, and his teaching I found astonishing.

When I came to the description of his celebrating the *Pesach*, or 'the Last Supper', I really asked myself, 'Who is this Yeshua?' The answer came a little further on in Matthew, when Yeshua was crucified and a sign was hung above him which said, 'This is Yeshua, the King of the Jews' (Mt 27:37). When I read that I was deeply moved, and put the book down. I asked myself, 'Why do they

write, "Yeshua, King of the Jews", and not, "This is
Yeshua, the false prophet", or "The false Messiah", or "the
blasphemer", or any of the other accusations that had been
brought against him? Why "King of the Jews"?'

I began to wrestle with God about the question 'Who is
this Yeshua and what does "King of the Jews" mean?' The
picture of Yeshua nailed to the cross, bleeding, suffering
and dying, with that sign above his head, 'This is Yeshua,
King of the Jews', remained with me.

Slowly the veil over my mind was drawn away and
suddenly I recognised Yeshua as my King, the King of the
Jews. I burst into tears, and sobbed my heart out. I couldn't
control myself any more.

This revelation completely overwhelmed me. From that
moment I was reborn. Just as with the birth of a baby, it
came about with pain and tears and emotion.

I cried bitterly for half an hour. When I was able to control
myself again, I continued to read the Gospel and came, to
my unspeakable joy, to the account of Yeshua's resurrection
from the dead. I knew nothing about it; it was completely
new to me. I read how the angel of the Lord descended
from heaven and said to Mary Magdalene at the tomb, '. . .
I know that you are looking for Yeshua, who was crucified.
He is not here; he has risen, just as he said' (Mt 28:5).

I was so happy that I danced around my room for joy.
He hadn't only died, but had risen again! I could do nothing
else but give my whole life over to Yeshua. There and then
I became his disciple.

I had no contact at all with anyone else. I didn't
even know if there were other Jews who'd had such an
experience. I thought that I was the only Jew who believed
in Jesus. For a whole year I kept this event to myself.

My brother lived in California and I finally went there
to tell him that I'd found the Messiah. I was very open
about it. I told him what I'd discovered. And my brother
came to know the Lord too. That is also very biblical: the

one brother who tells the good news to another, and leads him to the Lord.

At first my parents didn't know what to think about it. They didn't really understand what had happened to their two sons. But they did see the exceptional changes in our lives and that made them more and more positive about it.

The first time I met other believers was in California. At that time God was working there through his Spirit. The Jesus movement began on the West Coast. Of the hippies who came to faith in Jesus, 20 per cent were from a Jewish background.

Everyone who has found the Lord has done so in a different way. I don't believe I've ever heard a testimony which was like mine, about how Yeshua revealed himself as King of the Jews. Most Jewish people find Yeshua through the testimony of another Jewish or Christian friend. But with me it was without human intervention. God revealed himself sovereignly to me. Now, for the first time, the message rang out that a Jew could believe in Yeshua and still remain Jewish.

I had turned my back on Rabbinical Judaism when I was thirteen, but now that I'd found Yeshua, my lifestyle became more Jewish than before, as did my morals. My conduct became upright, and I began to keep God's commandments. That appealed in particular to my parents. They saw the changes in me and that made them envious.

In January 1974 I made the *aliyah* to Israel. During the early years I helped in setting up the congregations in Rosh Pinna and Tiberias and Nahariya in Galilee. In Netanya, at the house of the Messianic leaders David and Lisa Loden, I met my wife Pamela. We were married in 1982 and moved to Jerusalem in 1985 where we're going to stay until the Lord returns.

I have helped Pamela as her business manager, and she has helped me follow my calling to ministry as an elder in the congregation.

Pamela began to make more and more prophetic paintings in the 90s. She has started to paint what we, in Hebrew, call the *G'eulah Sh'leimah*, the full and final redemption of the Jewish people. In this work she follows the history of the Jewish people since 1930: first European Jewry during the Nazi holocaust, then the establishment of the State of Israel, the reunification of Jerusalem, and finally the end times and the return of the Messiah. It's a monumental work.

The final restoration of Israel is enacted in phases. In 1948 the State of Israel was established. God brought the Jewish people back to their land. After nineteen centuries of being scattered among the nations, they came back to their own country and began the restoration of Israel in their own God-given land.

In 1967, after the Six Day War, God restored the city of Jerusalem to his people. Yeshua said that Jerusalem 'will be trampled on by the Gentiles until the times of the Gentiles are fulfilled' (Lk 21:24). 'Trampled on by the Gentiles' means that the city is subjected to Gentile rule. In 1980 Prime Minister Begin declared Jerusalem to be 'the only indivisible capital city of the Jewish people for all eternity'.

At the same time God began to pour out his Spirit on many Jews around the world. I assume that this was a turning point, the first clear sign of the lifting of the veil, that is, the blinding of hearts towards Yeshua.

Now we're waiting for the third stage of God's *G'eulah Sh'leimah*, when God will take away the blindness with regard to the Person and work of Yeshua the Messiah.

Zechariah 12:10 says that God 'will pour out on the house of David and the inhabitants of Jerusalem a spirit of grace and supplication. They will look on me, the one they have pierced . . . and mourn for him . . . and grieve bitterly . . .' and he will 'open a fountain to the house of David and the inhabitants of Jerusalem, to cleanse them from sin and impurity' (Zech 13:1).

That is why I live and work in Jerusalem—to bring the gospel to the Jewish people and to pray for the salvation of Israel in order that we will see Yeshua as he really is.

For that we need revelation. Peter said about Yeshua, 'You are . . . the Son of the living God' (Mt 16:16), and Yeshua said that 'this was not revealed to you by man, but by my Father in heaven'. For a Jew, this is difficult to understand theologically. It will always be a mystery how God begot a Son, and he was born of the virgin Mary, and yet Father and Son remain one. But through the supernatural gifts of faith we can understand things which our natural understanding is unable to grasp.

It is particularly difficult for us Jews, who have the *Shema Yisrael, Adonai Elohenu, Adonai Echad*, to understand that there is a Father, a Son and a Holy Spirit. It can't be comprehended; we have to open our hearts to the revelation. God is lifting the veil of unbelief from the Jewish people.

Never before in history have so many books been written about Yeshua, nor have Jews said so many positive things about him. He is also the subject of a great deal of thought in Orthodox circles, as well as in secular ones. They say that he was a great Jew, a great rabbi and even go so far as to say that he was a great prophet. Recognising him as the Jewish Messiah is the next step in this spiritual development.

When he returns and his feet stand on the Mount of Olives, only then shall we have full knowledge of who he is. For me, Yeshua isn't only the Son of God, he is everything and all that the New Testament tells us. He is my Lord and Saviour, my King and Redeemer, my Bridegroom and my God.

We, as Messianic Jews, see it as our calling to develop an authentic Jewish lifestyle. It is an ongoing process which will combat the accusations which have been raised over the years about the Jews who believe in Yeshua, that they no longer behave as Jews and, in fact, aren't Jewish any more because they have converted to another religion. We have to develop an authentic Messianic Jewish lifestyle.

Messianic congregations must be planted throughout the country and we have to discover our own true identity. This process began in 1967 and we still have a lot to learn. But we are beginning to discover our Messianic Jewish roots, and we are going back to the first century to discover who we really are.

The reactions to all this have been many and varied. Some Orthodox Jews, who are blinded by their own prejudices, don't consider us to be Jews any more. Even if we were to keep the Law of Moses in the strictest possible way, they would still reject us as Jews. However, the secular Jews and even the atheistic Jews still see us as being Jews. It doesn't matter to them whether we keep the Law of Moses or not.

I really believe that we are living in the time when the spiritual blindness of the Jewish people is going to disappear. This is the next and most important step in God's plan for Israel.

Over the last ten years, so much has changed. A new generation has arisen. The new generation of *sabras* are now adults. The generation of Ben Gurion, Golda Meir and Menachem Begin has passed away and their place has been taken by the *sabras*, young Israeli Jews who have grown up in this country. They are less resistant to the gospel.

The generation that survived the holocaust and returned to this country came with deep wounds and unbelief. But their children have grown up in this country, and they see things differently. And this young generation is going through the same phases of development as the youth in other parts of the world. Drug abuse, alternative music, the search for truth, opposition to militarism—these universal youth problems also crop up here. I have been through them too, and I came out of them a believer. Hallelujah!

So I expect a great harvest over the next ten years! I do believe that Messianic Jews form a bridge between the believing Christians and the Jewish people. This is an important development in the history of Israel. Christians have a special responsibility to pray for Israel and to stand alongside the Messianic congregations. And the Messianic Jews are the natural branches which will 'be grafted into their own olive tree', according to Romans 11:24.

I would like to say to the Jews who read this and who still haven't found Yeshua HaMashiach that we have to put aside all our preconceived ideas and prejudices about who Yeshua is. We also have to put aside the history of the church for a moment and go back to the time before the destruction of the Second Temple.

The question is, 'Why was the Second Temple destroyed and why has Yeshua been made almost unrecognisable in Jewish history?' The only way to find out who Yeshua is, is to read through the New Testament for yourself, even if it's for the first time in your life. The biggest question is not 'Who is a Jew?', but 'Who is Yeshua of Nazareth?'

We have arrived at an important historical moment. Everyone is enthusiastic about the exodus of the Russian Jews and that is, of course, a great event in our history. But God's real purpose for the last days is the spiritual restoration of Israel, the final redemption of the Jewish people. That, and the breakdown of the wall of partition between Jews and Christians, is the deepest longing of God's heart.

His plan for Israel is that Israel should once again become a 'light for the nations' and a 'kingdom of priests'. Then we can fulfil our Messianic calling and represent God to the rest of the nations on earth. Then 'the law will go out from Zion, the word of the Lord from Jerusalem' (Mic 4:2). The nations shall then come up every year to Jerusalem to worship the Lord (Zech 14:16). In that day 'all Israel will be saved' (Rom 11:26).

2
Elhanan, the Artist

The taxi took me to Gilo, one of Jerusalem's beautiful suburbs. When I saw the white apartments spread across the hills, I was reminded of the text in the Bible which says that Jerusalem 'shall be built like a village'. I thought, 'How beautiful it will be here in the spring, when the purple bougainvillaea stands out against the white walls.'

It was a morning full of beauty and colour in more than one respect. The meeting with the artist Elhanan Ben Avraham (forty-five), and his wife Julie was refreshing.

Elhanan, with his slightly greying curls and his well-cared-for beard, first showed me a scrapbook containing photos of his work. A mural reminded me of my father's work, and I invited Elhanan to come and see my father's beautiful mural, 'The Source'.

I would hear that word 'source' many times that morning, as the greater part of Elhanan's life has been taken up with searching for 'the source'. He searched for it in many countries and had all sorts of experiences until finally he found God.

Elhanan invited me to take a seat in the *succah* on the

31

balcony, as it was the week of the Feast of Tabernacles. While we were talking, a soft breeze was blowing through the willow branches on the roof of the *succah*.

Julie brought out a bowl of assorted nuts and a carafe of fruit juice. Then we prayed. Elhanan prayed poetically that God would 'keep us in the *succah* of his peace'.

I belong to a Jewish family which emigrated to the United States from Hungary and Czechoslovakia. I was born in New York. After that, our family moved further and further west in the United States, just like many other families. After a while, we ended up in California, where I grew up.

You could call us an average Jewish-American family, conservative, but not Orthodox. We weren't over-religious and didn't have much knowledge of the Bible. But we were always conscious of being Jewish, although we couldn't grasp the depth of it.

I grew up with the feeling that I was always in the wrong place, and that I lived in the wrong time. I never really felt at home anywhere. Right from my earliest youth something wasn't quite right. The children I played with weren't interesting. Their jokes weren't really funny. The subjects which they talked about didn't interest me. Do you know what I mean?

When I was twenty-five—in the 60's—the world changed. Maybe it was God's Spirit being poured out, I don't know. During that period Jerusalem was also retaken; the Jews had waited 2,000 years for that. The hippie movement was in full swing and, in California, you had a front row seat.

Something was pulling at me, but I didn't know what. I felt completely detached from my own generation. I constantly thought, 'There must be something that's bigger than what I can see.'

The training for my *Bar Mitzvah* did nothing at all for me. I said, 'They only talk about God, but I don't see him.'

My parents suggested that I go and see the film *The Ten Commandments*. I was a twelve-year-old boy. Maybe the film would affect me and stimulate me to follow my lessons. We saw the film and I did indeed think it was fantastic. I was really quite moved and said, 'If there is a God then he's just like that.' But God wasn't as real in California as on Mount Sinai. I couldn't feel his presence and broke off the preparations for the *Bar Mitzvah*.

I also had my share of problems when I went to study art at university. I exhibited my paintings at an exhibition in the Brand Library in Glendale and that left me with some extra money. I said, 'I'm leaving. I'm going to buy a one-way ticket to Europe.' I put my tubes of paint and brushes in my case, and would see where I ended up.

In those days I'd developed a certain philosophy for myself which came down to, 'Up until now everything that people have shown me is a lie. Everything my ears have heard is in essence untrue. The only thing I'm sure of is that which my five senses can perceive for themselves. I can only believe what I see and experience.'

The most important part of my philosophy was, 'We have to go back in time.' In America nothing is more than 250 years old, and it is all packaged in cellophane—you can't even smell it. So, off to Europe! There you can go back in time; there you can at least still smell the baker's.

I arrived in Paris and could indeed smell the boulangerie from the street. I didn't want to be inhibited; I wanted to touch, feel, smell, see and experience everything myself. In Europe you can touch the walls that Napoleon once leaned against. In America you read about it in books; here you could feel it.

I lived in Paris for five years. I supported myself by making illustrations and I wrote articles and novels. I rented a beautiful studio near Ile Saint Louis.

I looked around in the countries round about me: England, Germany and Italy. Time and again I tried to go back into history. In Rome I experienced something of the source. Something began to grow in me there that would gradually assume a more definite shape. The Holy Spirit, who had been calling me from the cradle, filled me with longing.

I wanted to go back even further in time and travelled from Rome to Greece, the cradle of Western civilisation. I wrote down everything I experienced there, what I saw and heard. Later I was amazed at what I'd got written down on paper.

But I still hadn't found the truth. For the greater part of my life I'd been engaged in visual arts, but how could I paint the source if I didn't know where and what it was? Everything got in the way. Too much technique. Too many artists and fathers and mothers.

I was a lost soul, searching for itself. In Hebrew, sin is *chet*. That means something like firing a gun and missing the target. I was going in the wrong direction and missing the purpose of my life.

My life became sombre. Especially in the field of love. I was living an immoral life, but even that was a manner of searching. I sought after truth and love, but in the wrong places.

I was also barely aware of being a Jew. Someone asked me once, 'Are you a Jew?'

I answered, 'What is a Jew?'

Then that person said, 'Are your parents Jewish?'

I said, 'Yes.'

'Then you're a Jew. Don't you want to go and visit Israel?'

I replied, 'Never!' Israel was the very last place I wanted to go to.

I was working with a friend I'd known since I was five years old. He wrote books and I illustrated them. This friend suggested, 'Let's go to Brazil,' and I said, 'Why not?' Over the past five years I'd experienced everything you could experience in Europe, and I wanted to leave. The source wasn't in Europe, I knew that now.

We bought one-way tickets to Brazil, and there everything I touched came to nothing. In Europe everything had been successful, but now I'd turned to a new chapter and the blessings had gone.

First, there was the money. I had arrived earlier than my friend and ran short of money.

I found a flat and moved in, but I had underestimated the differences in culture. Brazil isn't Europe. As an American you can still be a bit at home in Europe. But Brazil is really another planet. It is primitive and sensual. The heat really knocks you out. There is no intellectual challenge and you just feel sticky and sweaty all the time. Everything revolves around emotions.

When I found this flat, it hit me straight away that there was a sticker on the door which read, *'Deos esta presente e vive Jesus,'* 'God is here and Jesus lives.' I opened the door—I still didn't know the *Ruach Hakodesh* then—and it was as if there was something in my heart which said, 'You're opening the door to a new phase in your life.' I stepped inside and I felt just like Alice when she stepped into Wonderland through the rabbit hole. I dropped into a thick deep darkness. From that moment, nothing went right any more. If I stretched out my hands to grasp something, it fled, and I was left grasping at thin air. I could not endure myself and I was terribly lonely. But even so, there was still an awareness, deep in my heart, that I was moving in the direction of the source.

I saw the primitiveness of unrestrained emotions. Western culture hadn't touched much here. Every inner urge was still expressed in its rough, rude form. In other words, I was still further back in time than in Greece; this was Africa. The African element is strongly present in Brazil, more than anywhere else in South America, and especially in Rio de Janeiro.

I kept at work on the book and while I was doing so, the figure of Jesus kept coming into the foreground of my thoughts more and more. In France I had written articles against Christianity and the churches in which I stood up for the Jew on the cross, who was misunderstood. Somehow I felt a bond with him: Jesus, the misunderstood Jew.

But religion didn't appeal to me; I was far too well aware of what was true and untrue, and I saw too much hypocrisy. In particular, I hated the way in which Christians and Jews condemned each other. You know how it goes: 'You mustn't talk to him as he's a *goy*,' and, 'You can't be his friend, he's a Jew,' and so on.

Whatever the cost, I wanted to find the truth, the source. No more compromises, no looking for a job or starting a family. How could someone like me bring children into a world like this?

Sometimes I would think, 'I'll become a respectable Jewish illustrator. But what is there to hold on to? This drawer might have a label but it doesn't even have a handle!' In every drawer I opened there was emptiness or just dusty books.

I felt like a fish out of water during those four years in Brazil. I saw things going on around me no one else saw. When I was on my way somewhere with friends I'd say, 'Did you see that, and that? That can't be a coincidence.' My friends called me the 'no coincidence man'. I would see a certain order, a cause and an effect, a plan. I just couldn't work out what the plan was.

I was thirty years old and already like an old man. I had seen it all and done it all. I found no hope in anything I'd read or seen. Were it politics or religion or art, nothing had any truth.

I realised that there were many artists who took their own lives, leaving a trail of pain with their friends. At the beginning of 1977 I had a dream. I saw myself standing next to a pond in a garden. It was a beautiful cool evening.

But a thick plate of glass with a small opening in it lay on
the pond. The water plants were pressing against the
underside of the glass. It was so beautiful that I took off my
clothes and dived into the water, through the opening in
the plate of glass. Only then did I realise that I wouldn't be
able to get any air under the glass plate. And while I was
swimming, I couldn't find the opening again. I had to
breathe, but I couldn't. That was the end of my dream.

But I didn't wake up. Straight away I had another dream.
I had completely forgotten the first dream, but was again
walking along the side of the pond. But now I stepped on
to the glass plate to see how strong it was. I saw that it was
holding under me and saw how beautiful the waterlilies
were as they pressed themselves against the underside of
the glass. Then, between the waterlilies, I discovered the
white, decaying face of a drowned man. When I looked
again, it was my face. Then I woke up, bewildered by the
dream. I thought, 'A person shouldn't have dreams like
that.' But later I understood the significance of it.

In January 1977 I went with some friends to the city of
Salvador to see the carnival there. In those days, the carnival
in Salvador was still primitive, not as commercial as in Rio.
The carnival was celebrated in the streets and everyone
joined in. Everything took place on the street: music,
dancing, using drugs, swearing and magic. Everything the
people have suppressed during the rest of the year comes
out then. The people are very poor there, but during the
carnival, they really live it up.

In those days God began anew to pour out his Holy Spirit
on me, which gave me the feeling that I was coming closer
to the source.

I had a vision that lasted for three days and nights. There
was practically no distinction between waking and sleeping
any more. 'There are only two possibilities,' I thought.
'Either this is the fulfilment of everything I have ever sought,
or there is only a satanic darkness without hope.' I realised

that there was no no-man's-land, no buffer zone in between; there was light and there was darkness. It was Bob Dylan who sang, 'You have to serve somebody, it may be the devil, or it may be the Lord.'

I was with my group of friends, meeting people, watching the carnival, but God spoke constantly. He spoke through the mouths of the people I met.

For the first time I began to be aware of my sinfulness. I realised that my sins had come to a climax. You put a seed in the ground, it stays there a while, it germinates, grows and then there comes a time that its fruit is ripe.

I also realised that sin is an infection that ultimately causes death. It was as if someone had turned on the light and a lamp had started to shine in a room full of rubbish. I couldn't bear it. I couldn't live like this any more!

A couple of small things still pointed in Jesus' direction and that gave me a special peace. For example, there was a girl wearing a silver chain around her neck on which hung a piece of jewellery containing a mustard seed. I asked her what the significance of it was and she told me about Jesus' parable. Faith is like a little seed with an enormous potency so that it can bring forth a big bush. I realised that Yeshua had said this 2,000 years ago. And this young girl in Salvador in Brazil wore a piece of jewellery that was a reminder of it. And I, a Jew, was touched by it. That word didn't touch my intellect only, but also my heart, my mind and my soul. It was really a living and active word.

The veil across my mind began to disappear and I could see clearly. The Bible tells us that this veil covers the thoughts of us Jewish people. It is just like the curtain which hung in the Temple, says God's word, between the holy place and the holy of holies and which was torn from top to bottom. All my life I'd been trying to tear that curtain from the bottom, but I had never succeeded.

Now God tore it from the top, and I suddenly saw all the fragments of my life—the times in Los Angeles, Paris,

Greece and Brazil. Different places and people passed the revue in my thoughts.

Suddenly my whole past folded out, like a scroll being opened. History went back into the past to my parents, and how their parents had come out of Hungary, and even further back to the land of Israel. Then I saw Zion, the city of the Great King, something which I'd never even thought about. I went back to Egypt, the Exodus, the patriarch Abraham. The scroll which had been rolled open was unbroken. All these things weren't just historic, but, even more, a spiritual reality to me. History came to life.

I had come to the point of confessing my sins. The Lord brought to my mind people whom I'd used. I had to weep for the friends whom I'd used emotionally. I had to ask for forgiveness from one friend who was with me. But he said, 'Oh, it's not so serious.' But I thought it was serious. I cried in front of my friends for it was my words that had hurt them, my actions that had wounded them. I couldn't bear the things the Holy Spirit was showing to me. I thought, 'Either I'm going crazy, or I'm meeting the living God.'

The friend with whom I was doing the book was a Christian, but he didn't practise his faith. He was worried about me. He went into the city and when he came back he said, 'Hey, I know that you're going through a difficult period. I've met someone who can perhaps help you.' I said: 'Who's that?' He gave me a note. I opened it and saw the name of a psychologist. His name was Dr Nazareth.

There it was again! Yet another indication that the only one who could heal my infection was the Man from Nazareth. Not this man from Salvador, who would probably give me some Valium, or pacify me with beautiful words, but the Man who died on the cross. So I said, 'Sorry, but I'm not going to the doctor.'

The Lord led me to the beach on the 'Baia de Todosos Santos', 'the Bay of All Saints'. It sounds morbid, but I now know that Yeshua also said that you can't be born again without dying first. That also comes to the fore in immersion. Of course, I knew nothing about that then. I lay my identity on the beach, by that I mean my wallet with everything I possessed in it, and ran into the water.

I felt as if I was coming close to the source, where my infection could be cleansed. The wonderful thing was that I really did have an infection in my foot, a symbol of the sickness in my spirit. I didn't want to infect people with my bacteria any more. It was a crime to continue to do that. I was sick of my paintings, my articles, of my way of mixing with people. I was so unclean before God, just like Isaiah, who said, 'Woe to me! . . . For I am a man of unclean lips, and I live among a people of unclean lips . . . .'

I began to swim in the direction of the ocean. I was ready to die. I thought, 'God may take me whenever he wants. I'm ready.' I was in fairly good shape and swam a kilometre away from the coast. But there was something special; it was just as if God was with me. I got tired, but he gave me new strength.

He led me to three volcanic rocks which lay in the bay. I climbed on to the middle rock for I was dead tired. When I had clambered on to the rock, I saw something remarkable. In that rock there was a hole through which the water from the breaking waves ran. The sound of the water running through was just like the flushing of a toilet.

I realised who these rocks were. I had climbed on to these rocks to become cleansed from my infection. I literally stuck my infected foot into the water that streamed away and felt the sickness pull out of me—something that was grainy and black and unclean. It was pulled to the depths of the ocean. I was overwhelmed and cried like a newborn baby.

After a time I swam back to the beach and had the feeling that God himself had baptised me. I had become a different person. My wallet still lay there, but the man whose passport photo was in the wallet wasn't there any more. Just like I'd seen in the dream. I looked down at the face of a drowned man, and that was myself. An exchange had taken place: Yeshua in the place of my old self.

It was unbelievable, but true. But it was also confusing and unclear; who could explain it to me?

Back in Rio, I found a Bible. I had very little knowledge of the Bible, but once I'd got hold of one, I couldn't stop reading it. For nine months I actually did nothing else but read the Bible word by word, page by page.

One day I read the text from Micah 7:19, 'You will again have compassion on us; you will tread our sins underfoot and hurl all our iniquities into the depths of the sea.' That was what had happened to me. I knew the Jewish use of *Tashlich*. On *Rosh Hashanah* we walk alongside running water, in prayer, to throw our sins into the sea.

I cried and cried when it hit me what had happened, and for the first time in my life I felt clean and light. I understood perfectly what Paul had meant when he said, 'I no longer live, but Christ lives in me.' He didn't say it lightly; he'd experienced it just like me.

One of the first things that God showed me directly, and through reading the Bible, was that I was a Jew. It was as if a voice inside me said, 'There you are then, the end product of a long history of Jewish people. You are united with the seed of Abraham. And even though I throw you into the greatest darkness and I scatter you throughout all the nations, I will find you again.'

I thought, 'Brazil is a considerable distance from Israel, but I have lived in great darkness and now I have to go and do something.' For Jews are called to make God's name known among the peoples. I still wasn't sure whether I wished to learn more about Jesus, but I liked him as a Jew.

I went on seeking in the Bible, from Genesis all the way through to and including the New Testament, and the feeling of time disappeared.

One day, when I read about the Day of Atonement in

Leviticus, I thought, 'Do you see that? It's the same picture—the one in the place of the other, the one dies and the other lives.' The exchange, this payment for guilt, the reconciliation. It was all so clear.

Then I felt led to go out into the street. I walked around for a bit, looked up and saw the Star of David. Just imagine, in the centre of Rio de Janeiro! What were all the people doing there? I walked up to a man and asked, 'What's going on here?' He said, 'Don't you know? It's *Yom Kippur* today!' I didn't realise that I was standing in front of the synagogue and that it was the Day of Atonement. God let me read about it in his word so that he could then bring me into contact with his people.

Later I visited the chief rabbi of Rio de Janeiro, as I wanted to find out about everything as quickly as possible. First, I had to get past a secretary. She wanted to know why I wanted to speak to the rabbi. 'Can you make me an appointment with the rabbi?' I asked, and told her that I wanted to speak with him about God. I was as naive as a child. She thought that I was making a joke and said, 'He doesn't speak about God.' Maybe she was right too.

Anyway, I met with the rabbi and let him read the Bible texts which prophesied that the Messiah was to be born in Bethlehem and had to suffer for our sins. He said, 'They don't refer to Jesus at all. You've got it wrong.' I began to discover that Jews are at least united in one thing: a Jew doesn't believe in Jesus. They are at odds about many other things, even about the question 'Who is a Jew?', but they are in agreement that as a Jew you cannot believe in Jesus.

I visited Catholic churches, Pentecostal churches and charismatic groups and tried to find out what was going on in them.

After two years, God confirmed to me something that

I, in my wildest dream, would never have expected: that I had to go to Israel. I read, 'I shall take you from all lands and bring you home to the land that I promised to your fathers.'

I set off on a journey again, first to the United States. There I told my family that I was going to Israel.

My mother is a dear, spiritual, eighty-one-year-old lady. My family have had their share of blessings and curses from the *Torah*, but my mother always stood firm for God. I told her about my experience and that I believed in Jesus. Then she asked, 'Have you become a Catholic?' I said, 'God forbid. I am a Jew who has found the Messiah. It's only now that I know what it really means to be a Jew. And I'm going back to Israel and I'm going to live there as a Jew.'

My mother looked around her in the room to make sure that no one could overhear and began to tell me about a vision she'd had many years ago. She said that she had been afraid to talk about it to anyone. 'I have also seen him,' she said. 'He stood here right in front of me: Jesus. His hands were outstretched and he was wonderful.' But then she said directly: 'Of course we are Jews, and we don't believe in Jesus, but he is a nice man. You can't have anything against him.' She saw that my life had been touched by God and she was happy about that. Later on she became a believer.

My mother did something else. She produced a yellowing piece of paper upon which something had been written in Hebrew on the eighth day of my life. I had received it at my circumcision thirty years before. My Hebrew name was on it.

Back in Rio, I took it to the synagogue. A man explained to me: 'This is the name that you received at your circumcision, Elhanan. That means "God has forgiven, God has been merciful".'

Isn't that miraculous? That piece of paper with my new

name had been lying waiting for me for more than thirty
years. I had never been happy with my English name.
Just like everything else it was wrong. The wrong place,
the wrong time, the wrong name. A drawer with a handle,
but nothing in it. Elhanan—God had forgiven me. This was
the name for my new life. I had been born again and I was
free.

While I was in Rio it just happened that the Jewish *Pesach*
and the Christian Easter fell at the same time. I went to a
Baptist church, but some of the people turned their heads
away when I, the Jew, walked in with my mulatta girlfriend
at my side. There was still a lot about me which had to
change on the outside even though God had touched me
on the inside.

I met other believers and we went to a party given by
the marines the evening before *Pesach*. We were all old
friends together but strange things happened there. While
everyone was dancing and drinking, I went on to the
balcony and began talking to friends about God. I'd never
been to a Bible college or anything like that, but suddenly
I had an enormous knowledge of the things of God. My
friends looked at me strangely, and some realised that there
was something special happening to me.

I had to leave everything behind and by grace I did that,
and flew to Israel.

But the empty drawers kept on following me. I can't help
it, but whenever I come into a room, I always pull open
the drawers to have a look inside. Handles are nice, but
they have a purpose: you have to pull them. Many people
find them just nice to look at, but I want to grasp them to
see what's in the drawers.

I began to ask questions again. I spoke with the Orthodox
Jews and asked what it meant to be a Jew.

I said, 'God has not brought me back to Jerusalem to
become a Baptist!'

I went to study Hebrew. I already spoke Portuguese,

French and English. But Hebrew is as deep as the ocean. The other languages are the waves on the surface.

I asked some Christians, 'God has commanded the children of Israel to keep the Sabbath, why don't we do that?'

They answered me, 'That was done away with by Christ. We have now entered the Sabbath of Christ.'

I replied, 'That sounds good, but it also says, "For all your generations!"'

No one could give an answer to this question. Again, a drawer with only dust in it.

Just after my arrival I met my wife Julie— in the cotton fields between the kibbutzim. Precisely as someone had prophesied, I met my Ruth in the fields in Israel. We married, and she was the woman of my dreams; we had two children.

One Sabbath morning, while living at an absorption centre in Jerusalem, I started my car in order to go to the Baptist church. Everyone was at the synagogue or asleep; it was perfectly still and the noise of the engine starting tore through the silence.

I went inside again and said to Julie, 'I think that we should honour the Sabbath.' She said, 'But the fellowship with other believers is also important.'

So we did go to the service, but the thought wouldn't go away. Finally I said: 'After today we keep the Sabbath. God will provide if we keep his ordinances.'

So we lit candles on Friday evening, said the *Kiddush*, the blessings for the beginning of the Sabbath, and felt that we had done something that God asked of us.

Our neighbours from the absorption centre, whom we hardly knew, looked in; they saw the candles and said, 'Hello!' We said, 'Oh, please come in and be our guests.'

They came in and a conversation developed. Then they looked at the bookcase and saw a book about Yeshua. We thought: 'If only this could end okay!'

Then my wife said suddenly, 'We are Jews who believe that Yeshua is the Messiah.' I gave her a kick under the table to make her stop, but the big word was already out.

And do you know what our guests said? 'So do we!'

So God immediately provided for our need of fellowship with other believers when we were obedient.

We met even more believers, invited them along, and so within one and a half years had formed a home group. I played the guitar when we sang together. We didn't have much knowledge, but we did have a lot of enthusiasm.

I had to find someone who could answer my many questions. Some questions I didn't dare to ask of the believers I met. They were too afraid of them.

Then I met a man, Joseph Shulam, who knew the *Talmud* and the New Testament. He wasn't afraid of questions. If he had a giant in front of him, he would slay him, lay him on a table, cut him up in pieces, pull out his intestines and say, 'What was I afraid of?' I am now a part of that Messianic Jewish congregation here in Jerusalem.

The Messianic movement has its childhood behind it and is now in its puberty.

We are somewhat like the returning salmon, which swims upstream until it reaches the upper course of the river where it was spawned. That involves swimming against the current.

If you want to have it easy, it may be better to stay in America. Then you can be a Messianic Jew with a *kippah* on your head and a King James Bible under your arm. That is *gefilte fish* Judaism—cosmetic. It may be another form of entertainment.

When I came here twelve years ago, I had to cry a little every half hour. I put my hand in the Israeli soil and thought, 'Earth and flesh have become one.' Suddenly I realised, 'I'm in the right place, at the right time and now I have the right name.'

I went to the Western Wall and heard God say to me, 'Welcome home.'

I have come home after a long, long journey.

3
Sha'ul, the Fisherman from Galilee

We are sitting in an idyllic place, Sha'ul Zuela and I, shielded by bushes, with the clear running water of the Jordan at our feet. Sha'ul has a bearded face, piercing eyes, gesticulating hands. A man who fears nobody.

Into my mind comes a picture of Peter, the disciple of Jesus. Peter was a fisherman on the same Sea of Galilee. And Sha'ul used to go fishing too. Peter was a powerful personality, a born leader, with a kind of roughness, stubbornness even. The same can be said of this modern-day apostle who sits beside me.

I know that sometimes Sha'ul can be unco-operative and difficult to handle. But today this lion is a lamb, friendly and patient. I need to change the batteries of my cassette recorder and Sha'ul says, 'Take your time.' Today he is full of laughter—a roaring, free, extrovert laugh that scatters the white herons further down the Jordan. Sha'ul laughs away the persecution of the Orthodoxy that tried to stop the Messianic congregation; that tried to close down the Galcom-factory which produces radios for missions; that sought to end the Galilee Experience—a slide presentation

51

with an inbuilt testimony of Jesus; and to shut the primary school. This laughter may raise hell, but Sha'ul does not care, because God showed him in one of his incredible dreams how demons are paralysed if rebuked in Yeshua's name.

While Sha'ul told me his story, my mind went back to two years ago. My wife, Wiesje, worked as a television presenter, and Sha'ul gave his testimony on her programme. We were deeply touched. Here was a Jew, right from the shores of the Sea of Galilee, who saw the name of Jesus written in the sky without even knowing what it meant. He found the Lord in a supernatural way!

We decided to go to Israel and search for more such stories and write a book of them. And God turned our lives upside down with a Messianic glow. All that is very biblical: if these modern disciples of the Jewish rabbi Yeshua cross your path, you will no longer be the same.

I was born in 1951 in a tent. The little town where I spent the first years of my life is called Hadera. It lies on the shore of the Mediterranean Sea. My parents were among the many immigrants arriving in the land at that time. There were no houses for people to live in so they lived in tents. Housing was just as big a problem then as it is now. Israel, at that time, was a very young state.

My parents came from Iraq, that is, biblical Babylon, where Abraham came from. They were Orthodox, so I grew up in a religious environment. But most Jews from Iraq had problems concerning their faith. They thought that the truly great rabbis were in the land they had left. The biggest *Yeshivas* at the time of the Second Temple were in the land that is now Iraq. But here in Israel they did not have much influence.

My father was disappointed by the religious life here and by many other things. But still he kept up the traditions.

I was a happy child. Almost every day I went with my

father to the sea to catch fish on which we lived most of the time. The economic situation was so bad, we had little else to eat.

I used to walk alone to the synagogue, a two-minute walk from our place. I had six brothers and sisters and we were a happy family. There was a loving atmosphere at home. My father and mother never argued with each other. And in a tent you cannot hide an argument! Later on we moved to a very small house with only two bedrooms. But even there I never heard my parents fight or shout at each other.

My father was the authoritarian figure in the home and my mother brought loving care to the household. My father always backed my mother. If she said something, it had to be done.

I was the naughtiest child of all. I encouraged the other children in the neighbourhood to have fun. Sometimes we slaughtered the neighbours' chickens. We did this because we saw the rabbi do it. Already I was the leader of the group, to my sorrow I must add.

In the synagogue I heard what the elderly people had to say about God and the Scriptures. And there the problems arose. For they dealt more with the *Halachah*, the traditions, than with the real Scriptures. Of course, in the synagogue we read the Law of Moses, a number of the psalms and some of the prophets, but most of the time we were dealing with the words of man.

But still I knew from a very young age that God was my Father. My grandmother actually taught me, 'God is the Father of the Jews.' And I believed that. I used to have conversations with God. I looked up to heaven and spoke to him about things that made me happy or sad, in a childish way.

But I also began rebelling against the religious establishment. I went to school and started to read and write and found out that what was taught was not always from the heavenly Father, but was just religion, just tradition.

They said, for example, 'If you go to the sea on the Sabbath you will die.' But I thought, 'If God is my Father, and if I go with him to the sea, just as I go fishing with my earthly father, I won't die!'

One day I put this to the test. It was the Sabbath and I went to the sea and put one foot in the water. I did not die. I tried the other foot. Nothing happened. Finally I walked into the water so far that I could start swimming. Again nothing happened.

The next day, Sunday, I went to school and we had religious instruction. I said, 'Teacher, can I say something?'

He said, 'Please.'

I said, 'Yesterday I went swimming in the sea.' Everybody froze. I continued, 'You told us, teacher, that if we went to the sea and swam on the Sabbath we would die. I did not believe that God would do something like that. So I wanted to try. I put one foot in the water and did not die. To make a long story short: I put my whole body into the water and I am still alive!'

Of course they kicked me out of the school and it created a big scandal.

My experience of God continued with two dreams I had at that time. I would dream about the end times, what would happen in the future. And I would dream that I met father Abraham, and Moses who taught me the Law, the way he saw it. I have adored Moses since then. He was the most loving man you can imagine. From that time on Moses was a special man for me.

Reading the Bible, and discovering God's caring love, gave me more and more problems with these hard laws that were taught. I found that the rabbinical teachings add to the laws of God to such a degree that it turns people from the Lord.

One day I decided that I did not want anything to do with that kind of teaching. I thought, 'If I follow the Bible in the way they teach me I am cursed, and if I don't follow it, I am also cursed.' I said, 'God, I cannot live this way, but I know you are my Father, and I wait for the Messiah, and I know that you have a special call for me. But I will go away from here and live in a secular kibbutz where they don't want anything from God.'

I moved to a kibbutz in the north of Galilee, and kept believing that God was my Father and that one day I would see the Messiah and be changed. But who was the Messiah beside the fact that he was the son of David?

I did not know anything about Christianity. In my thinking, everybody who was not a Jew was a Gentile and they were very different from us. They didn't have God, or any future. I had never heard of the New Testament.

When I was thirteen I started to go to high school and lived the normal kibbutz life. But I continued to have dreams. And I continued to be convinced that God was my Father, and that the Messiah must come, that our lives would need to be changed and that there was a destiny for the Jews and a calling for us.

Then I had to go into the army. I served as a paratrooper and was stationed in the Sinai. I was on my way to my base and the assembly point for our unit was the central bus station in Tel Aviv. We usually gathered there and would go from there to the borders. Politically it was a very hot time. Some things had happened at our base by the Suez Canal that I cannot talk about.

I was walking to the main street leading to the central bus station when suddenly I looked up into the heavens and saw a name in large flaming letters of fire, magnificent and powerful. Those letters were big and alive. They were red and orange in colour, like fire. I know I was not imagining it for I was not thinking about anything at that moment. What I saw was the name of Yeshua in Hebrew, and I knew at once that this name was the name of the Messiah.

I felt so small that I wanted to hide in a crack in the road. Where could I hide from that overwhelming name? I was filled with awe. Then it disappeared. But I could not tell anybody about it. I had a lot of questions: 'Who is Yeshua?' I did not know anything about Yeshua. I knew only in my heart that this was the Messiah, the Son of God. He was God himself.

I did not know anything about Christianity. Nothing. Nobody had ever told me about Jesus. As a Jew, you don't mess around with Gentiles.

I went to my base in the Sinai. Days passed. But I never could forget what I saw.

When I met Zahava, my wife, a *sabra* from a kibbutz near Tel Aviv, I said to her, 'Look, if you want to marry me, you must understand that one day God will use my life to serve him. I believe in God, although I am a sinner. I believe in God and in the coming of the Messiah and I am his servant. I will walk away if he calls me. So if you want to marry me, you must take this into consideration.' She said, 'I want to marry you because I also believe in God.' She too had a lot of questions arising from her observation of religious life, but in spite of them she had a desire to serve him as well. I said, 'Good, then we can marry.'

We lived close to Mount Hermon in the north. The place was called Rosh Pinna. One day I came home from my work. It was cold and rainy and I sat near the fireside and read the Bible. Our Bible has a different order. First there are the five books of Moses, followed by Joshua, Judges, Samuel and Kings. Then Isaiah, Ezekiel and the minor prophets. When I read from Genesis to Kings it would be fine, I could understand everything. But when I started to read the Book of Isaiah I would fall asleep. Every time I opened Isaiah, I would fall asleep, without fail.

So the first miracle happened: I opened the Bible at Daniel and I began to understand. Even the Aramaic part, for a part of the Book of Daniel is in Aramaic. I said to my wife, 'Zahava, come over here and look what Daniel is saying: a son of man will come out of the heavens on the clouds with all authority, and everything will be given unto him. That must be the Messiah.' And I thought back to the vision I had had, how I had seen the name of Yeshua written in the sky in letters of fire.

I continued to read and started to study Isaiah and did not fall asleep. A few words touched me deeply: that God does not want our sacrifices or our feasts, because of our iniquities: 'So wash yourself to be pure and remove all this uncleanness.' I thought, 'He is calling us to repentance.' But repentance was not what I saw in the religious life around me.

Then I had three dreams! One of them was about the end times, the persecutions that will come. People will want to kill us because we believe in God and follow the Messiah, and we will run away into the wilderness where God will give us food, and so on. Later on I saw that all that was recorded in Revelation 12, the story of the woman running into the wilderness.

In the second dream I saw the sun being extinguished and the moon turning to red. In the dream I saw the moon broken in pieces on the great day of the coming of the Lord. Many believers were waiting for the Messiah to come and were building the tabernacle of David. I said, 'Come, let us build the tabernacle of David because he is coming. The Messiah is coming!' Everybody took a piece of wood and shouted, 'We are going to build the fallen *succah* of David. Yes! If the Messiah comes there will be a tabernacle!' And we were tremendously excited. I woke up from this dream full of expectancy.

The third dream came the following night. I was in the wilderness and every grain of sand was golden. I was wearing jeans and a wet shirt. I was sweating and dirty. That was a time when wearing jeans and having long hair was a sign of rebellion. In those days you were not allowed to go to school in jeans and with long hair!

I was dirty because of my sins and I said, 'O God, I cannot stand myself. I am standing here in this vast wilderness and I don't know what to do.' Suddenly a voice came from heaven. God himself, the Almighty, said, 'Soon your Lord is going to appear and when he comes, you will go to him and say: Speak Lord, your servant is listening.'

As I heard the voice of God saying that I thought, 'Goodness, the one I am to see must be the Messiah, for these words are written in the Bible and were spoken by Samuel when he heard the voice of the Lord.'

Then I was reminded of God's visitation to Abraham in Genesis 18. Abraham saw three men coming; one of them was the Holy One and the others were angels who wanted to destroy Sodom and Gomorrah. Suddenly, from out of the heavens, three persons appeared, one each side of the one in the middle. They came down from the blue sky, over this beautiful golden sand, and flew about three metres above the ground. I ran to them and bowed my knees before them and said, as God had commanded me, 'Lord speak, your servant is listening.'

I was in a state of shock. I could not utter any other words. The angel at one side had blue garments, but they were transparent—you could see his shoulders, arms and hands. I saw his ankles and feet on which were something like sandals. The other angel was identical to him. He had very beautiful curly hair. But his garments were of a different colour—red. His arms and his face and feet were like those of the other angel. They paid no attention to me. All their attention was on the one in the middle. They did only what he told them to do. They stood shoulder to shoulder with him; they were cleaving to him.

I was looking at them and two things made a deep impression on me: their obedience to him and their power. They were mighty and strong. I knew that if I did something wrong, they would consume me before I could move. They gave glory to nobody, except the middle one. Their only focus was on him.

Now I looked at the middle one. It is difficult to explain. His body was covered with a beautiful white garment. I could not see any part of his body. The garment reached the ground, and covered the ground around him. You could not see his feet. His hands were in the sleeves of the garment. I could not even see the palms of his hands. Of his face I could only make out the eyes, nose and beard, nothing more. On his head he had a beautiful white turban, like that of a high priest. A golden band covered his forehead, but nothing was written on it.

I thought, 'This is interesting. The high priest was dressed like this, but he had a text on his forehead: "Holy unto the Lord." But this person does not have this, because he is the Lord.'

Then I had another thought: 'What happens if I look into his face? Will I die?' I decided that it was worth dying for, so I looked into his face. He had friendly eyes. And out of his mouth came incredible words. His voice! Oh, his voice is impossible to describe. It was so beautiful and powerful. Like the rolling thunder. No other voice is like that. It vibrated and the whole world echoed. All the strings in the world vibrated with it. Yet you could hear clearly what he said.

He was speaking in a language I could not understand. The words came out of his mouth like giant letters. Each letter was taken and put aside, and then another letter came out and the angels put it next to the others to form a word. When the word was complete it was placed on one side, and the same with the next word. Whatever was spoken was a testimony in the heavens. These were giant letters, burning with fire, like those I saw written in the sky above the bus station—ancient Hebrew letters, like those I had engraved on my ring. Here, look at the ring with the words 'Yeshua, the Servant, the Alpha and Omega'. I was fascinated.

There was also a pleasant smell, and when he spoke the whole area was cleansed. I was cleansed too from all my weight of sin and all the problems that I had in those days. They were all solved and vanished. He was cleansing me, and I knew that the role of the Messiah was to do that.

I saw everything, things that human beings cannot see, in another dimension. I saw him speak, that was the most important thing. And all the while the angels stood there, transfixed. They never moved their heads, as if they did not care about anything. I thought, 'They must be fascinated too.'

I woke up from the dream, but without the garbage of my sins. I told my wife what I had seen and said, 'The time is coming when we will see the Messiah. And he is far greater than anybody says. What people say about him is nonsense. He is more than anything in the world. I am going to see this Messiah coming.'

Three days after that I met a friend, who had just been fired from his gardening job. I said, 'Come and see me and I will find you a job.' At that time I worked for an insurance company.

He replied, 'You don't need to, God will take care of me.'

'What do you mean,' I asked, 'by "God will take care of me"?'

'God is my Father,' he answered.

I said, 'Yours too?'

He looked at me and repeated, 'He is my Father and will take care of me.'

I said, 'Come, I have to tell you something.'

So I started to speak with him and share my Messianic hope and the visions I had seen.

He said, 'Yes, of course you saw Yeshua. I am a believer in Jesus.'

'You're crazy, we are Jews,' I replied. 'What you tell me belongs to the Gentiles.'

He contradicted, 'No, you don't understand what you saw. It was Yeshua and he is written about in the Bible. I am ready to sit with you and read the Bible with you.'

He was a good friend of mine, but I had not known he was a believer. Had I done so, I would not have spoken with him.

I accepted his invitation. He began to explain that what I had seen was a description of Yeshua HaMashiach. He read a psalm with me, then he invited me and my wife to come the next Sabbath to talk further.

We had moved from the kibbutz to an apartment in Rosh Pinna and had brought some boxes of books with us. All kinds of books—cheap novels, but also very serious books, and Bibles. Those orange boxes full of books were piled up on the balcony.

One day I was sitting on the sofa, telling my children a story. The first-born was four years old, or less. My second child was two years old.

Then my four-year-old shouted: 'Dad! There's something behind your shoulder! Don't move, Dad! It's coming closer to your shoulder!'

I said, 'What is it?'

'A scorpion!'

I moved aside. There, on the back of the sofa, just a few centimetres away, was a black scorpion with big claw-like pincers, its poisonous tail ready to strike. Just as it was ready to strike me, I killed it. Its body fell between the sofa and the wall, so I moved the sofa away and there I saw another scorpion. It ran away and I chased it through the house to the balcony where all the boxes from the kibbutz were stored. I saw the scorpion crawling into one of the boxes. I turned the box over. But it had gone. I turned over another box and another and another. Nothing! Finally I saw the creature disappearing down the drain hole.

I returned to the hall but what was I to do with this

chaos? I decided to make a library for the books. The next day I created a bookshelf by welding together pieces of metal and put all the books on it.

Now, I had a bad habit. I am rather ashamed to mention it. You see, I was kept very busy repairing electrical appliances for poor people. I would help large families with several children that had no money, and would do the repairs for free. However, sometimes too many would come to see me, especially when I had just arrived home from work. So I would give my wife a kiss, make a cup of coffee, take a book and go to the toilet to escape. There I would smoke a cigarette, drink my coffee and read my book. That was my bad habit.

My wife would always say, 'You are disgusting.' But I would retort, 'You clean the toilet every day, so I sit in a clean place and nobody can tell me to come out.'

On a certain day I came home from work and hurried to the toilet. I took my cup of coffee, just grabbed the first book I saw, went into the toilet, shut the door and started to read. It was the New Testament! I opened it and started reading Matthew 1:1, 'This is the genealogy of Jesus Christ the son of David, the son of Abraham.'

Jesus! But that was the name I saw written in letters of fire in the heavens! He was the Messiah, the Son of God! That was incredible! And I started to read and read. Then I turned to the epistle of John and to my amazement I read, 'In the beginning was the Word, and the Word was God. He is the light of the world.' If this book I had in my hands was not a Bible, then what was it?

So I went on reading and saw Paul's description of Jesus as the High Priest. And I thought, 'That is the man I saw in the vision and he cleansed me from my sins. That is the role of the Messiah.'

I read on and on in the toilet and did not realise that the time was passing. My wife knocked on the door and asked, 'Are you still alive?'

I said, 'Of course I am alive! But don't disturb my reading.'

She retorted, 'You have been inside so long. Don't you think others need to use the toilet too?'

I said, 'You don't believe that I am reading.'

'You're crazy,' she replied and left.

After that I spoke to my friend and said, 'I don't know what book that is, but I can tell you the writer describes what I saw written in the heavens, and the man I saw in the dream, and I know it is the Messiah.'

He said, 'Sha'ul, that's a New Testament you have read!'

A Christian lady must have put it between my books in the kibbutz, for all the Bibles we received were cut open, the New Testament was taken out, and then they were glued together again.

I said, 'Come with your wife and talk with me and my wife, because you are the only Jew I know who believes in Jesus. If he really is the person I saw, then I will be the second Jew that believes. Together we will be the only Jews in the world that believe.

He replied, 'No, there are more Jews than you think that believe in Jesus.'

I asked, 'Are you sure about that?'

'I am sure, and they have a meeting on Saturday. I'll take you up there.'

I said, 'Okay.'

Rufen and Benjamin Berger and Shmuel Suran lived together at that time in Rosh Pinna, the place where we lived, though we did not know them. My friend took me to their house. I told them what had happened to me at the bus station and about the dreams and Rufen said, 'You have seen the Messiah.'

I said, 'I want you to prove that to me. And why don't our rabbis believe in him?'

I had a lot of questions about the Gentiles and this and

that. I made it hard for him. But he opened the Bible and started to read from the prophets.

I told him, 'You don't have to read any more. You don't need to convince me, because what you say is true.' I hugged him and said, 'I'm happy that I have found my brothers.'

There had always been a desire in me to meet real brothers. Even at the time we did not know the Lord I would say to my wife Zahava, 'One day we are going to find real brothers, who love God and love one another, and share their lives with one another.' Now I had found them.

Two weeks later my wife also had an experience of the Lord. She received a prophecy and a dream. First she experienced the presence of God in the house, and then she had a personal meeting with Jesus. She experienced him in the spirit. It was like a wedding.

I could not wait to be baptised. But the brothers said that many things in my life needed changing, and so one month later we were baptised in the upper part of the Jordan near my kibbutz. Now I understood the cleansing power of the Messiah I had experienced the day I saw the vision. It became a reality for us both.

I told God, 'You promised me that you would work in my life, so now I will give you all of my time.' I quit the job I had and continued to help people, repairing washing machines and speaking to them about Christ. I had taken a course in electronics and could make a radio, that was almost all. But I would pray that the Lord would give me wisdom and knowledge if I needed to repair something, and he did. I always did this without asking for money.

Then God showed me that I should leave the place where I lived, Rosh Pinna, and go to another place. There I met Ken Crowell a brother who wanted to start an electronics factory and I was the first worker to join. I said, 'I will work with you for half a year and will leave you then, because God has a calling for me.' God had shown me that through the story of the children of Israel who broke up their camps and moved onwards.

Now God spoke to me again, 'Move ahead!'

My wife and I prayed, 'Lord, give us another believing couple,' and a couple arrived, new immigrants from America.

We prayed, 'Lord, we want to open up a fellowship. Not that I wish to be a leader, but I want there to be a body of believers in this town.'

One week later I made contact with a brother from America and we started to meet every Tuesday night for Bible study. At that time there was no organised fellowship in the city. There was only a meeting on Sundays in the Scottish church. But I am a Jew and I don't go to church on Sunday. So we started to pray and slowly, slowly, the Lord started to bring people.

Then I told my brother, 'I want to go fishing. Would you like to come?'

He replied, 'Yes. I'll buy a boat.'

So he bought a small old boat and we started fishing on the sea of Galilee. I said, 'David, I now know how we can build a fellowship.'

'Tell me.'

'Let's go and give every believer enough fish to feed his family.'

'Okay, let's pray.'

We prayed, 'God, we don't know how to fish, give us fish.'

We caught some large carp and cut them into 200-gram pieces. We discovered that we had enough fish for every family. Of course it was foolish, because if you calculate the cost of petrol for the boat you could have bought this amount of fish for the same price. But we did it for the Lord and the plan worked: the following Tuesday night my house was filled with people.

But my house was in the old part of Tiberias, where all the religious Jews lived. They knew we were believers for

I used to go and preach the gospel carrying a big bag on which was written in big red Hebrew letters: 'Jesus Christ is the Son of the living God and I am his servant.' I would go into a shop and buy a pencil or something cheap, because I did not have much money, and the people would ask me questions and I would give my testimony.

Meanwhile, 'number four' was born—a daughter— and the house became too small for the family and the fellowship. So the believers started to meet instead in the home of two Dutch midwives, Annie van der Weg and Lidy Verkruisen. They had rented a huge house. Later on the group appointed elders and I was one of them. I served in this role for about nine years or more.

During these years the Lord taught me how to cast out demons. In a vision he showed me what happens when demons are rebuked in Jesus' name. They become frozen and cannot move any more. They are chained, paralysed. The Lord said to me, 'That is all you need. You have authority in my name. Don't use gimmicks or special methods, just rebuke them in my name and they will become paralysed.'

On another occasion the Lord taught me about the heavenly language. As I lay in bed at night two evil angels wanted to kill me. My heart stopped beating and I saw myself from afar, lying in bed beside my wife.

I prayed, 'Holy Spirit, the word of God says you are interceding for the believers with groans that words cannot express. So please, Holy Spirit, I don't understand what is going on, and am willing to go to my heavenly home, but not with these ugly creatures.'

And then the Holy Spirit spoke from Psalm 124:7: 'We have escaped like a bird out of the fowler's snare; the snare has been broken and we have escaped. Our help is in the name of the Lord, the Maker of heaven and earth.'

Suddenly there was a fire from deep inside, and the Holy Spirit spoke from within me in a heavenly language. And

. . . it was the same language that Jesus had spoken in the dream. It was so mighty that those two evil creatures vanished like sparks. Gone! Then a blanket of heat came over me. My heart began to beat normally and I could move again.

I woke my wife and asked her, 'Do you know what has just happened?'

She replied, 'No.'

I said, 'That's strange. I thought the whole universe would have heard that voice, it was so loud!'

She assured me, 'Chatsy, I didn't hear a thing.'

Now we have nine children and are still serving the Lord. The congregation is strong and can continue without me. The factory, too, is a success, and provides employment for many immigrants, among others.

But I want to open up new fields and dream of a school, somewhere here in Galilee, where we can train people to be intercessors for a spiritual breakthrough in the land of Israel.

4
Joseph, the Theologian

The newly formed Messianic congregations in Israel need a theological backbone, which is why God has given them Joseph Shulam.

● Someone has to take the time to put into words what characterises this movement.

● Research has to be done into the situation of the Jews who believed in Yeshua in the days of the first century.

● Commentaries must be published that do justice to Jesus as the Jewish Messiah and yet are still acceptable to the general public in Israel.

● The Messianic congregations have to be autonomous. This movement isn't something fostered from the outside, a church founded by missionaries, but an authentic expression of Jewish belief in the Messiah.

Joseph Shulam and his friends set up Netivyah for this purpose. They hope one day to be able to publish a complete Hebrew commentary on the New Testament.

I looked Joseph up in the Netivyah building on Narkis Street in Jerusalem, not far from Baptist House. A great battle has been fought for this building, a square block two

storeys high, built of white stone. Before Netivyah could
take possession of the whole building the Orthodox fellow
residents first had to be bought out. It seems that every step
that the Messianic believers take is accompanied by a battle,
just as in the time of Joshua, who took possession of the
Promised Land.

It wasn't easy to make an appointment with Joseph. He
is a very busy man who has given lectures in Finland, Spain,
England (in Oxford!), Greece, Japan, Hong Kong and the
United States. Joseph's wife is called Marcia. His son Barry
is twenty-one and is studying to be an engineer in the USA,
and his daughter Danah is nineteen and is an officer in the
Israeli army. Joseph speaks no fewer than seven languages—
Hebrew, English, Bulgarian, Spanish, Arabic, German and
Russian!

While telling his story, his hands move over the keyboard
of his ultra-modern computer. A *curriculum vitae* rolls out
of the printer. A little while later a 'short history of Netivyah'
appears, and as we talk about theology, a 'profession of
faith' rolls out.

This place is one of the focal points of the Jewish Messianic
movement. Here the special role of the Messianic Jews and
their message is being thought through at a scholarly level.
In other congregations emotional experiences perhaps play
a greater role. Here people want to know, understand, study
and share.

I was born in Bulgaria in 1946. My parents came to Israel
in 1948. They entered the country legally, as Bulgarian Jews,
which was exceptional in those days. You see, the situation
in Bulgaria was unique.

When Jews from all over Europe were dying in the
extermination camps, there were hardly any Bulgarian Jews
among them. The reason was Rabbi Daniel Tsion, who
believed in Yeshua. He had received a vision that if even
one Jew was taken away from Bulgaria by the Germans,

the Czar's entire family would be killed. With that vision he went to Czar Boris Kobourgotsky, who listened to him.

The Czar made an agreement with the Germans, allowing them to occupy Bulgaria without any opposition if they undertook not to expel any Jews from the country. The Germans agreed to this condition, with the intention of breaking the agreement later anyway. However, the Bulgarian people managed to prevent it. There was no anti-Semitism in Bulgaria.

In 1947 Ben Gurion and Teddy Kollek visited Bulgaria and told the Jews of their plans to establish a Jewish state. All 75,000 Jews then wanted to emigrate. In 1948 the State of Israel was declared and in the same year 50,000 Bulgarian Jews entered the country.

My parents were among the first group. They were still very young and I was only twenty months old. My father had worked with the Allied command after the war. When he arrived in Israel, he got work straight away because he could speak several languages. He first worked at the Spanish consulate and, after that, with the Israeli government.

I can't remember anything about Bulgaria because from the age of two I grew up in Jerusalem. I had no interest in religion, or anything related to it. My mother was a communist and my father an atheist. He hated religious people, Jews as well as Christians. The terms he used for them were 'primitive, superstitious, under-developed people'. Belief in God and in the Bible wasn't modern.

But he was a nice man and everyone loved him. If there was a feast in the synagogue, someone's *Bar Mitzvah* or another special occasion, then they always invited my father. My father didn't care and would cheerfully enter the synagogue with a lighted cigarette on the Sabbath.

So I have a totally unreligious Israeli background. When I went to secondary school I read the Bible for the first time.

It was a semi-Orthodox secondary school and one assignment the teachers gave us was to write an essay about the
beginnings of Christianity. We had to analyse the religion
with regard to its form of government, structure, holy days,
and most important dogmas. For this I had to read at least
five or six chapters of the New Testament, the Sermon on
the Mount and the first chapter of the Book of Acts.

I got my hands on a New Testament and what I read
appealed very much to me, as a secular Israeli. It dealt with
problems such as hypocrisy, violence, misunderstanding
between people, religious disputes—problems which crop
up again and again in Jerusalem. The New Testament
surprised me because it was so Jewish. I looked up
Christianity in the Hebrew encyclopedia and was again
surprised as it seemed to talk about something totally
different.

As I read the New Testament, I couldn't find anything
Christian in it, at least not according to the norms which
the teachers had given us. I didn't find priests, nuns,
convents, Rome, Protestants, archbishops or Christmas in
the New Testament. I didn't find any of the Christian holy
days; on the contrary, everything was very Jewish. That
surprised me greatly, and aroused my interest.

I wanted to discover exactly what had happened in
history to have caused the division between Judaism and
Christianity. I read every book about Jesus that I could get
my hands on. I asked my teachers what literature was
available and read many Hebrew books. I spent a year
reading and studying.

In the middle of that year I met an American family who
lived in the same neighbourhood as I. They had children
who were my age and a big American car. I was especially
interested in the children, as they had American toys that
no one else in Jerusalem had, and the daughter was pretty.

I played with the children and became good friends
with them. I used to attack the children verbally, saying,

'Christians don't do what their own Bible says. Christians don't keep holy days like Jesus did. Christians have Christmas which isn't in the Bible.'

One day the father came to me and said, 'Why do you attack my children's belief and tell them that they aren't Christians?' I explained that I had read the New Testament, but that what I'd seen of Christianity didn't tally with what I'd read in the Bible. He said, 'You're right!'

We became friends. I travelled around with this man to translate and do other things for him.

But after a couple of months I thought, 'I must be crazy. I'm spending all my spare time with these Christian people while I'm not even a Christian.'

But the following day I thought again: 'And what if Jesus really is the Messiah? Maybe Jesus really does give eternal life and forgives sins!'

All these questions went through my mind, until a day came when I'd had enough of it. I couldn't stand my own contradictory thoughts any more and began to cry. I decided, 'I'll turn my back on this whole business and forget Jesus and Christianity. What do I get out of it anyway? It's an obsession and it's of no use to me. I need my time to study and I'd like to play with my friends in my spare time.' It was 10 o'clock in the morning when I came to this conclusion.

But by 1 o'clock I had swung around totally and said, 'If Jesus is the Messiah, and it says so in the New Testament, then I'd better look into the matter seriously.'

My American friend was in hospital, so I went to another friend of his and told him, 'I want to be a disciple of Jesus.' I already knew that you had to be baptised in order to be a follower of Yeshua. What did I have to lose? And, what could I win?

The missionary took me with him in his car and we drove to the Mediterranean Sea, a little to the north of Tel Aviv, where I was baptised.

It was an intellectual decision, not an emotional one. Every emotion was against it: my upbringing in the city of Jerusalem, the atmosphere at home, my friends and the roots of my culture. I gave up everything that I had learned as a Jewish Zionist child. Becoming a Christian meant roughly the same as being a man from Mars. It would have been easier to fly to Venus than to become a Christian.

It was a difficult decision, but it was a logical conclusion after reading God's word. As Paul says, 'Consequently, faith comes from hearing the message, and the message is heard through the word of Christ' (Rom 10:17).

In the preceding months I had read ten books about Jesus in Hebrew, both for and against him. In the previous two years I had read the New Testament three or four times all the way through. I hadn't once read the Old Testament, only the New. And the question that was constantly before me was: how is it possible that such a Christianity could come into being from these Jewish doctrines in the New Testament? I just couldn't understand it.

After the baptism we came back to Jerusalem and I was dropped off at my house. When my parents heard what had happened, that I'd become a believer and had been baptised, they threw me out of the house.

Now the military barracks from the time of the war of independence are still standing in Jerusalem, between the railway station and the Hebron Road. A part of these barracks, which were built by the British, is used nowadays as a police station. As boys we often played in these barracks. We had our huts and hiding places up in the attics. It was our own kingdom. We formed gangs with groups of young people and played war in and around the barracks. So when I was thrown out of my house I went there and found a place to sleep in one of the attics.

I was sixteen and had a lot of friends. We were at a rebellious age so I didn't care too much about being thrown out of my home. I ate with friends or with the missionaries and still went to school and didn't really feel abandoned at all.

But on the fourth day after my baptism my parents went to the head teacher of my semi-Orthodox school and told him what had happened. I knew that this meant that my education at this school was over.

That same day I went to a church service and met Joe Grey, an American tourist. He said to me, 'I'm going back to America now and will send you a ticket by post. You can use it to come to America as we have a good boarding school in our city. You can finish your education there.'

And it actually happened. A couple of days later I received a ticket and flew to America.

I not only finished my high school education there, but carried on to study at Michigan Christian College.

During those years in America I didn't have any contact with my parents. Sometimes I was very sad about this, but I continued to write to them, even though I never got a reply. I wrote to them every month but never received a letter in return.

When I was at university, the missionary with whom I first had contact in Jerusalem came back to the United States and he telephoned me. My mother had had an accident at work and was seriously burned. That had happened shortly after I had left Israel. She'd been lying in hospital for two years.

Immediately I broke off my university studies and went back to Israel. Arriving in Jerusalem I got in touch with my father at once. He was with my mother in the hospital. I went there and they received me warmly.

My mother had had plastic surgery many times for her extensive burns. Shortly after that my mother returned home and I visited my parents again at home.

I didn't know if there were any other Jews who, like me, believed in Jesus. If so, I longed to make contact with them and tried to bring this about.

I continued my studies at the Hebrew University and
worked in the evenings. I made a living from odd jobs.
Sometimes I was able to translate for the preachers.

In my one-room flat, students and believers met each
other. It was a meeting place for young people from all
kinds of groups. The first few Messianic believers came to
my flat and we became a congregation automatically.

As a Jew I didn't feel right with the Baptists or the
Pentecostals or any other group. I wanted to stay a Jew and
an Israeli, but in the Christian churches a different culture
ruled. They sang old-fashioned English hymns which had
been given Hebrew words, such as 'Onward Christian
soldiers' or 'A mighty fortress is our God'.

If someone came into church with a *kippah* on his head
they made a big issue of it. Today you can hardly believe
that that was how it was twenty years ago. They forced
you to take off your *kippah* or else leave the church.

It was impossible to be a Jew. They didn't keep a single
one of the Jewish holy days, and were continually speaking
out against Judaism. They shouted from the pulpit, 'Aren't
you glad that we don't live under the law any more, that
we don't need to keep the Sabbath any more? Aren't you
glad that we can eat pork?' That was the atmosphere in
these churches.

If we witnessed to our friends about the Messiah, we
couldn't take them to such a church, where they shouted,
'Hallelujah, we are believers and eat ham sandwiches,' and
where they sang Protestant hymns.

After the Six Day War I returned to America to round
off my study of the New Testament, because you couldn't
do that here in Israel.

When I came back after that, I met Marcia and we got
married. In 1972 we went to live in Jerusalem and visited
a certain church. The preacher gave bombastic sermons in
a church where there were only fifteen people.

Half of these people were totally off their rockers. We

have a large number of people in Jerusalem who are off their rockers. For example, there were three women in the church with the name of Miriam. One of the three Miriams was 'Miriam with the dogs'. She had roughly twenty dogs and they followed her all over the city. When she went into church the twenty dogs stayed outside the door whining and barking. She always stank of dogs. Then we had 'Miriam with the flowers'. She always sat in the middle of the first row, right in front of the speaker, and had a big rose or a carnation in her hand. During the sermon she waved this flower and heaved long heavy sighs. And we had 'Miriam with the problems'. She had the habit of always coming forward so that the preacher could pray with her. You could never say anything about it; it went with the church.

I felt that I needed to know more about Orthodox Judaism, having been brought up in a non-Orthodox family. My parents were, after all, a communist and an atheist. While we were beginning to build up a congregation here, I studied at the rabbinical seminary and completed the course in two years.

We wanted the congregation to become a congregation like those of the first century, and Israeli in nature. That's why we studied the New Testament teaching on the relationship between the law and the gospel, grace and good works, conversion and the Jewish-Christian relationship.

We were continually asking ourselves, 'How can we be faithful to the New Testament belief?' My work was therefore twofold: on the one hand studying, and on the other helping people to find their Messiah.

In the ten years that we built up the congregation in that way, innumerable Jews as well as Arabic people came to belief. As time went on, hundreds of Christians and non-Christians visited the congregation and received help in different ways. Many lives were changed by Jesus as people found 'the way of the Lord'. We also established an Arabic congregation alongside two Jewish ones.

In 1981 the organisation Netivyah, 'the way of the Lord', was set up. It was necessary to form a legal foundation, if only to have such things as a bank account. Netivyah has as its goal to study and teach the word and to bring it to life in the church according to the model of the church of the first century.

In 1983 there wasn't a single place in Jerusalem where Israeli Jews could come together in an environment of their own to hear about the Messiah of Israel. If a Jew wanted to know more about Yeshua, he had to go to one of the established churches. But many didn't fancy going to the local Catholic or Protestant church. They would rather not be seen in such a church.

On 11th April 1983 we signed the contract, after ten years of wandering around like nomads. We had had meetings in parks, in houses spread across Jerusalem or in rented church buildings. And that in the city where, 2,000 years ago, the church of the Lord had begun!

Now we finally had a place where we could come together and worship, and could study fearlessly as Jews. The number of visitors grew to sixty and quickly doubled, and now there is standing room only.

More than nine languages are spoken by members of the congregation. The Lord has made our congregation a blessing for the whole world. We distribute a quarterly magazine, *Teaching from Zion*, that is sent to more than twenty countries.

Netivyah has become a model of a pure Jewish congregation, just like those in the first century here in Jerusalem. Various organisations and study groups have evolved from us.

Joseph and David Stern became joint leaders. Dr David Stern made an important contribution to the discovery of the Jewish Messianic identity with the writing of the 'Jewish New Testament'. He translated the New Testament from the Greek in such a way that the Jewish element was preserved. More books, such as *Restoring the Jewishness of the Gospel*, helped to lower the threshold for Jews looking for the Messiah.

Then problems came from a totally different direction than we had expected. The owners of the building broke the rental agreement. We believed that the Lord had given us this building and therefore wanted to buy it so that no one could ever throw us out again, but the cost was £125,000. We prayed to the Lord to provide for this need, and God heard. The money came through gifts from the United States, Finland, and from all over Israel.

We then had to help the four families who lived in apartments in our building to move. That also cost a large sum. The last apartment became vacant on 1st September 1990. It had been occupied by an Orthodox Jewish family, which had caused us many problems in the past. That cost another £94,000.

Now, at last, we were the owners and the only users of this building and we could start doing it up. Downstairs we furnished a beautiful auditorium with blue chairs and artistic decorations on the wall. We also have verbal permission from the local authority to build an auditorium on the roof with seating for 200 people.

One of the most important projects which we have begun is called *Rabbi teach us*, a Hebrew commentary on the New Testament. For this project we want to work with professors from the Hebrew University to produce for the general Israeli public as objective and acceptable a commentary as possible.

God is again building his congregation in Jerusalem. We are a small group of pioneers and suffer many restrictions. But we have started the work, building on the promises of the Lord. Jerusalem is a difficult place in which to proclaim the word of God, but God's plan is being worked out and cannot be stopped. 'For Zion's sake I will not keep silent, for Jerusalem's sake I will not remain quiet, till her righteousness shines out like the dawn, her salvation like a blazing torch. The nations will see your righteousness . . .' (Is 62:1–2).

We believe that Jesus is both God and man. In the Bible Jesus is depicted as the 'Son of the living God'. It is said of him: 'There is no other way to the Father but through him.' Jesus is the only source of salvation for the whole of humanity. But, God is one.

This dogma is not just icing on the cake. A Jew is prepared to die for his belief that God is one. Anything that diminishes this is idolatry and cuts a person off from the worldwide brotherhood of Jews.

The rejection of Israel as God's chosen people is a persistent dogma in most evangelical circles. This dogma is directly opposed to the distinct teaching of the Holy Scriptures, such as Paul's teaching in Romans 11.

The majority of Christians consider there is an antithesis between 'grace' and 'following the *Torah*'. But Yeshua's teaching is perfectly clear in relation to grace and the law: salvation comes from God through his grace and all our works are like dirty rubbish. That does not mean, however, that a child of God can withdraw from keeping the law and thus not obey it. Judaism in its present-day form as a system and as a persuasion has moved away from Moses on certain points, but the *Talmud* and the Jewish literature are still a part of our heritage and we must maintain respect for them.

The land of Israel also has a biblical significance. At a time when many Christian theologians adhere to 'replacement theology' (which proclaims that the church has come in the place of the Jews as God's people), it is necessary to point out that the land of Israel occupies an important place in the New Testament.

God's plan for the present, past and future is not separate from Eretz Israel. We teach members of our congregation that the family life of the Jewish believers must reflect the belief in Jesus as Messiah and that the family home must

be a place where Jewish people are welcome. The house of
a believer in the land of Israel must be such that a moderately
Orthodox Jew can enter and eat at the table with ease.

Jesus said that our justice must surpass that of the scribes
and the Pharisees. That doesn't mean that we are 'under
the law', but it means in practice: live as the Jews did in the
first congregation.

5
Menahem and Haya, the Pioneers

Jaffa Road, in the centre of Jerusalem, is noisy and dirty. Buses fight their way through traffic and the pavements swarm with people of all nationalities and colours. A small market is literally black with Orthodox Jews buying *lulav* for the Feast of Tabernacles.

If you watch, you can see how carefully the men inspect the palm, myrtle and willow branches before they buy them. In particular, the *etrog*, a type of lemon, is subjected to a painstaking inspection, as everything has to be perfect for this joyous feast.

I find the building where Menahem Benhayim works. Taking the elevator, I quickly reach the office of the International Messianic Jewish Alliance on the eighth floor, and find room 844. I knock on the door and hear a lively voice: 'Come in.' Menahem welcomes me with a big smile and Haya offers me a seat.

As I am getting out my camera, the sound of a siren screeches through the air. An ambulance or police car? In Jerusalem you often wonder: has a bomb exploded?

Above the noise of traffic, I listen to the fantastic story

of these pioneers. Twenty-nine years ago, in March 1963, Haya and Menahem Benhayim came as immigrants from America—they were the first American Messianic Jewish couple to settle in Israel.

They have seen with their own eyes how the small trickle of water in the desert has grown into a river; literally in the desert, for their story begins in Eilat, the southernmost settlement in Israel.

Who better than they can indicate the dimensions, the content and the future prospects of the Messianic movement in Israel?

Haya is a typically American Yiddish *memme*. She speaks in long-drawn-out sentences with large gestures, but also as one totally convinced of the truth. She is a motherly type, despite the fact that as a result of her pioneer existence she has never had children of her own—but she and her husband have been mother and father to innumerable young people. I listen to her first.

When we came to Israel in 1963, we didn't know what awaited us. We hoped for the best, and were prepared for the worst. In our kibbutz I had to clean the toilets and do all sorts of other heavy work. Coming from a well-to-do family, I wasn't used to that at all!

I had Jewish ancestors on both my father's and my mother's side. Imagine it, my grandfathers were called Abraham and Isaac, and my father's name was Jacob.

I grew up in Connecticut in the United States in a traditional Jewish home, where a girl doesn't have much to say. When I was seven I met a Swedish girl at primary school. Her mother was a very spiritual lady who knew the Bible well. She told me about God and about Jesus. But I thought, 'I'm the youngest of seven children in a traditional Jewish family, this is not for me. My mother and father, older brothers and sisters would never accept it if I believed in Jesus. They wouldn't even listen to me if I tried to tell them.'

It was many years later, while I was staying with my
married sister in Florida, I was lying out on the veranda
and I had a vision. I saw myself falling into a bottomless
pit. I was falling, falling, going faster and faster. It was dark
all around me and I thought that God was punishing me.
I was convinced that I was lost because of my sin. I had
read the Old and New Testament, so I knew something
about God's judgement.

It was a terrible experience and it frightened me. So, for
the first time in my life, I called out to God. I cried, 'God,
have mercy on me!' And it was as if a ten-ton weight
had been lifted off of me. Afterwards, I felt light and
peaceful, and had to laugh and cry both at the same time.
Since then, I've met other Jews who have also had such an
experience—but back then, I thought I was the only one
on earth.

Miami Beach in Florida was also called 'Little Israel'
because so many Jews lived there. The Swedish people from
Connecticut had told me that there was a small mission for
Jews close to the beach. They said that I'd be received with
open arms should I ever go along.

I felt I couldn't go to a church, for, being a Jew, you are
always reminded of 2,000 years of church history. If you
believe in Jesus then you're not understood in the synagogue
either. Messianic Jews can be very lonely.

The mission was led by two older ladies. They gave all
the Jews who came there Bibles and good evangelistic
literature, and invited them to come to the meetings.
When I went in a hymn book was pressed into my hand.
That was the first time I'd experienced anything like that.
They sang 'Sweeter as the years go by' and I thought it
was wonderful and I volunteered to help them in their
work.

When I was twenty-one, my father died, and four years
later so did my mother. My mother was always worried
about what would become of me, as I had led a loose life.

But through that vision, and because I surrendered to God, my life changed.

I prayed for ten years for a husband and in 1961 I met Menahem. He had become a believer several years earlier, and had been baptised by immersion in water. We married in the house of a believing Jewish couple in Connecticut, and we became very active witnesses among Jews and Gentiles.

In those days, we were often the only believing Jews in the surrounding area. There was no movement of the Spirit among the Jewish believers as there is now.

Before our marriage Menahem had gone to all sorts of meetings and people sometimes looked at him very strangely, as if he was a sort of curiosity. Yet Jesus and all the apostles were Jews and the Bible says, 'For salvation is from the Jews' (Jn 4:22). For us it was like the Dark Ages, a time in which there was only a tiny remnant of Messianic Jews.

Now it's Menahem's turn with his story.

I, Menahem, Ben-Hayim, am the youngest child of Hyman and Rebecca who emigrated to the United States from a village in Eastern Europe at the beginning of this century. The area in which they lived was part of the Austrian empire, but after World War I it was incorporated into Poland.

They both grew up in a Chassidic Jewish community, where little had changed over the centuries. For them the move to America meant a lot of adjustment, but they tried to hold on to as many of their old traditions as possible. Together with their seven sons and daughters—me being the youngest—they lived in a crowded tenement house in New York's Lower East Side.

My father was a simple tailor, who spoke only Yiddish. From the age of ten he had to work to earn money as his parents were very poor, and therefore he'd not had much education. He knew only Jewish prayers and traditions and he insisted that these were strictly observed, at least at home.

My mother wore a wig in accordance with the Chassidic Tradition. But in America more and more Orthodox women did away with the wig—they found it too old fashioned. After my father died my eldest sister finally succeeded in persuading my mother to let her own hair grow and put away the wig. The children became more and more American. By the time I was old enough to go to school, our family had climbed a little further up the economic ladder and we could leave the unheated tenement house in the ghetto. We could afford a flat in Brooklyn with central heating and an inside toilet.

Because a lot of Italian immigrants lived in this district, I had the idea that the world was made up of two races—Jews and Italians. Once, at the age of six, I was walking home from school with my Italian friend and we were talking about religion.

'Pasquale, did you know that our God created the world?' I asked. I had only just heard the Genesis story of creation.

My young Roman Catholic friend searched for an answer. After he'd thought for a long time, he said, 'But our God created the streets.'

After this heavy theological dispute we continued our way home in silence.

Most young people had to go to work as soon as they could leave school. It was the time of the great depression. Hitler was a rising political figure and the communist and socialist parties were very active in New York. Many young people who were non-practising Jews were attracted to the radical political movements.

Cheder, the Orthodox Jewish school that Jewish children attended in the afternoon after normal school, was still very old fashioned, especially when my brothers went there. There was very little to make Judaism appealing, and everything was said in Hebrew and Yiddish. The children didn't like it.

When I had reached the age to go to the *Cheder*, I met a more moderate form of Judaism. An attempt had been made to get along with the children in a more constructive manner. They tried to awaken our interest. We had lessons in Hebrew, Jewish national history, social history, and Zionism.

That was a bit better than what my brothers experienced, as they had to learn by heart endless prayers which they didn't understand. They were treated in an old fashioned way and as soon as possible they turned away from Judaism.

My mother had a few demands to which the children had to agree: such as attending the synagogue on the high Holy Days, taking part in the Passover Seder, and having strictly Kosher food at home.

Most Jewish children of that generation turned their backs on Orthodox Judaism. They thought it was something from the old world and that there was no place for it in America, the new world. Meanwhile we were conscious of the threat of an enormous tragedy developing in Europe. We saw the rise of anti-Semitism, and even in our American surroundings there were Nazi-like groups.

When I reached the age for *Bar Mitzvah*, I was being pulled in many directions. On the one hand I found some modern forms of Judaism attractive, and on the other I was being pulled towards the secular and non-religious movements.

While I was in high school there was quite a controversy in our Jewish community about a book—*The Nazarene*—written by the Yiddish writer Sholem Asch, which was translated into English. The writer, coming from a Jewish perspective, was very sympathetic towards Jesus and his followers, whom he described. The book was a bestseller in America and stirred many Jews to think about the Jewish Jesus–Yeshua.

In a synagogue I sometimes attended for late Friday evening services, the rabbi discussed the novel in two lectures. Many Jews had attacked Asch, angry over his sympathetic description of 'Rabbi Yeshua', while others commended him because he wanted to show Jesus as a good and faithful Jew. I felt that I had to read the book too, but had no money to buy it. I couldn't borrow it from the public library either, as it was constantly out on loan. I often thought of it over the next few years.

In December 1941, America became involved in World War II, and I was called up in March 1943 for military service. They tested me and I did well in the IQ exam. Therefore I was sent to a medical unit for training and was later sent off to England as a medical orderly.

For several months I was stationed near Barnstaple, a quaint village in Devon. I hadn't forgotten *The Nazarene*, and I thought that Sholem Asch could help me to understand this strange man, Jesus of Nazareth, who shone as a bright light in the history of mankind. But I did feel that I must first study the source of the novel—therefore I decided to read the New Testament before I read *The Nazarene*, now available to me in the base library.

I went to a bookshop in Barnstaple at night because I didn't want anyone to see me. Everything was blacked out because of the German bombings, so I could buy a Bible unseen. It worked. I found the shop and bought my first complete Bible, in the Authorised Version. Also, I didn't want my Jewish comrades to see what I was doing, so I read the book in secret.

And what I read touched me deeply. I read the Sermon on the Mount and Jesus' parables, and a great joy came over me. This rabbi from Galilee spoke the truth, I thought, and I learned whole sections of the Gospels by heart.

I was especially struck by how humble Jesus was and

how he taught the disciples not to seek honour or status. I read Matthew 20:25–28:

> You know that the rulers of the Gentiles lord it over them, and their high officials exercise authority over them. Not so with you. Instead, whoever wants to become great among you must be your servant, and whoever want to be first must be your slave—just as the Son of Man did not come to be served, but to serve, and to give his life as a ransom for many.

I found this to be compatible with the best Jewish thought. What objection could a thinking Jew have against this? Also, what a difference from so much of the Christianity that Jews had known!

The archaic language of the King James Bible didn't hinder me, as I was used to reading good English literature, even Shakespeare, for pleasure.

I was convinced that, if there was a basis for the Jewish Messianic hope, it lay with our own Rabbi Yeshua, 'from whom men hide their faces' (Is 53:3).

I had also hidden my face from him. But more and more I came to the conclusion that I couldn't escape him. I sensed that I would have to commit myself openly to Jesus. I knew that I wouldn't be any less a Jew if I did that. It would rather be the fulfilment of my being Jewish, a 'circumcision without the use of people's hands'. Still, it was extraordinarily difficult for me, as Jewish life and culture were deeply rooted in me. In the eyes of most Jews, such a step meant that you cut yourself off from your own Jewish heritage.

In the American army I was surrounded by Protestants, Catholics, and several evangelicals. Some only went to church because it was wartime and they were afraid. After the war I came into contact with liberal groups where I felt more at home, because there I didn't feel threatened by Christian symbols and dogmas.

For a while, doing good works appealed to me very much. I was active in the conservative Red Cross, as well as in the socialist 'Catholic Worker', a pacifist-socialist movement which did a lot for the poor and destitute in New York.

I was energetic, interested in everything that went on around me, read a lot, and wrote articles for an inter-racial paper in New York. But I only shared my faith in Jesus in private discussions. I was always careful not to appear too 'religious' among my mostly liberal and secular companions.

In England, I had visited the great cathedrals of the Church of England and was affected by the beautiful artistry and the music. I was still conscious of the fact, however, that I was a Jew, and Jews don't belong in a church except as visitors, I thought.

Two years after coming out of the army, I had a remarkable experience. I went to buy the Passover wine for my mother from an Orthodox Jewish shop on New York's Lower East Side, where they had the strictest kosher wine. My father had died the year before and I was expected to lead the family *Seder*. As it was a beautiful spring day, I walked the several miles from my Brooklyn home.

Along the way, two New Testament texts came to mind very forcefully. One of the texts related to the challenge of Jesus to the rich young man: 'Sell your possessions and give to the poor, come here and follow me.' The other was from the Sermon on the Mount: 'Don't worry about tomorrow, as each day has enough trouble of its own.'

I thought, 'This is the way I should go to follow Yeshua.' I decided to give away all my belongings directly after Passover. My mother was a widow and she would get it all. Then I would leave for a destination as yet unknown. In 1948, the same year that Israel became a state, I literally sold everything, collected my personal savings from the bank—some 250 dollars—and gave the money to my mother.

I decided to look for work in the shipping industry. I visited shipping agents along the East Coast of the US, and I heard about a United Nations ship that was leaving Brooklyn. Because of my military medical background, I was signed into a transport which collected displaced persons from Europe and shipped them to countries offering asylum around the world. On board I would work in the hospital, or on deck when there were no patients.

At one point on this journey I sank into a deep depression, which reached its lowest point when the ship docked in Bremerhaven in occupied West Germany. I felt abandoned, and was deeply troubled. I even prayed to God that I might die. I took a trip to Bremen and saw depressing bombed-out ruins all around.

Back in Bremerhaven, hundreds of refugees who were to be transported to South America began to embark. Because I knew Yiddish, and could also make myself understood in German and had learned Spanish, I had much work as a translator. In addition, I helped the sick and worked in the ship's hospital kitchen. The work was invigorating.

After just one day I felt like a new person. I realised that God was at work in my life. I had reached my lowest point, and was now moving upwards.

I eventually returned to New York, and sometime later met a Jew who believed in Yeshua. He was Rachmiel Friedland, who worked among Jews in the Lower East Side. He came from an ultra-Orthodox Jewish family from pre-war Poland and had come to believe in Yeshua in Warsaw in 1937. His whole family was later destroyed in the Holocaust, but he miraculously survived.

Rachmiel put me in touch with other Jewish believers, and I got along with him very well. We often spoke to each other in Hebrew and Yiddish, and I could relax with him, without the theological and cultural problems one faced with non-Jewish Christians. Most evangelical Christians whom I met weren't socially involved, and they didn't care much about the racial conflict in America. They only spoke about being 'saved' and going to heaven, or they confronted you with pat questions about the Trinity.

In 1960, I asked Rachmiel if he would *mikvah* me, or immerse me. I didn't want to be *mikvah*ed in Christian church surroundings, but in a Jewish context. My substitute for the Jordan River was Coney Island in Brooklyn, a very Jewish area. Rachmiel introduced me to the Hebrew Christian Alliance (now Messianic Jewish Alliance) and I met other Jewish believers.

On New Year's Day, 1961, I visited the Hebrew Christians of Bridgeport in Connecticut, and there I met Haya. Later that year we were married in the house of some Jewish believers.

A year later we moved to Miami Beach in Florida, and I went to work as an orderly in the Jackson Memorial Hospital. We were happy as there was freedom to speak about our belief, and our lives were full of activity.

We both had a deep love for Israel. In my youth, I had already been active in the Zionist movement which then strove for the founding of a Jewish state in Palestine. Nevertheless, as believers, we felt we weren't strong enough to settle in Israel.

Many Jews were convinced completely that the Christians were our greatest enemies. In their way of thinking, the Nazis were Christians, and Messianic Jews were traitors who had gone over to the enemy camp.

But the thought of going to Israel kept working in us. A year after our wedding, we decided to ask God for a sign. We got the sign and in March 1963 we went on board an Israeli cargo boat which took us from Miami to Israel.

We went as tourists and stayed a few weeks with the

Friedlands, who had emigrated earlier. We looked around, and went to work for several months in a kibbutz. Later we helped Rose Warmer, a survivor of the holocaust, who distributed Bibles throughout Israel.

After that, we established ourselves in Eilat, where we applied for permanent resident status. Eilat was then a small settlement, trapped between the Negev Desert to the north, the Sinai desert to the south, the Red Sea to the east, and the Arabian port Aquaba. I went to work in the port as a docker. Working in the heat of Eilat was heavy going, but I was in my thirties, so I was strong enough.

My colleagues couldn't understand that I, being an American, worked so hard—most of the Americans they knew were rich tourists. Many of the oriental Jews in particular could not understand—they very much wanted to move to America or Canada, but I had come from there to toil in the heat and dust of Eilat!

After the Six Day War I found employment with a shipping company where I worked for ten years.

During this time we held house meetings and distributed Bibles. Haya was especially busy with the many people who came to visit and slept on the bunk beds we had in our small flat.

More and more English-speaking people came to Eilat. It was the time of the hippies. They lay on the beach all day and smoked hash or worked as casual labourers. John Pex, a Dutchman, was one of them. We were able to help him in his journey to faith.

I began to write again in various Christian, as well as Jewish, periodicals. In 1976, the International Hebrew Christian Alliance asked if I would be their Israel secretary. Rachmiel Friedland and his family had moved back to America. I accepted the offer on a part-time basis, but gradually it became too much, working hard all day in the office at the shipping company, writing for periodicals and representing the Alliance. So in August 1977 I gave up my job and in November we moved to Jerusalem.

The Messianic movement was developing rapidly. More young people were coming to faith, and the influence of the American 'Jews for Jesus' became noticeable in Israel. We received wide coverage from the media.

In 1974 I became a member of the Lausanne Committee on World Evangelisation, and in 1977 I was invited to serve on the board of the Bible Society, and helped to found the Messianic Alliance of Israel.

The Messianic Jewish Alliance seeks to link Jewish believers from all congregations with each other. Many Messianic believers still don't feel accepted in Israel. We flutter around, like a bird which hasn't yet learned to fly. We haven't developed strong wings with which we can rise like an eagle. The problem is that we're still such a mixture. Don't forget that every Jew has a different background. In the congregations are Jews from the Yemen, India, South Africa, Ethiopia, the British Isles, Eastern Europe, and North and South America, as well as native Israelis. Israel is a huge melting pot. At the same time our congregations still maintain many of the characteristics of the churches with which they have been in contact in the diaspora, or through which they came to faith, including the way in which they conduct worship. We have charismatic and non-charismatic evangelical free church, liturgical and others.

Often it's strong personality which keeps a congregation together. Sometimes the problems are not on a theological level, but concern the personality of the leader. This has occasionally hindered the growth of the Messianic Jewish part of the body of Christ in Israel.

Therefore the Messianic Jewish Alliance, on the basis of the teachings of Paul in Ephesians 2, wants to bring Jews and believing Gentiles together while respecting their under-lying differences. We want the Jewish element to be restored to the church. In his time Paul fought the Jewish leaders who felt that Gentile believers had to be circumcised. He taught that Gentiles could keep their culture and lifestyle, as long as they weren't in conflict with the Scriptures. They could even eat meat at a pagan feast as long as they did not offend other believers.

God didn't want the Gentiles to be cut off from their own roots. And Jewish believers clearly remained within their Jewish context. Paul and the other apostles lived a Jewish lifestyle but at the same time were connected with the vigorously growing church of the Gentiles.

The tragic thing is that somewhere in history, the Jewish element was driven out of the church and died. And in the synagogues there was no place for Jews who believed in Jesus the Messiah. We have 1,600 years behind us in which being a Jew meant *not* being a Christian, and being a Christian meant *not* being a Jew.

It is only recently that this situation has begun to change. The monopoly of the church as well as the synagogue has been broken. It has been made possible for Jews and Christians to live and believe in a New Testament way. Now it is possible for a Jew to remain a Jew as he believes in Jesus, and for Christians to leave space for the special identity of their Jewish brothers and sisters.

Few Jews have found in the country from which they came, be it America, Sweden or Holland, a place where they could express their faith in a truly Jewish way. Here in Israel this is gradually happening. We have grown in number. It is difficult to state how many Messianic Jews there are in the country, because most congregations are mixed. In some groups only half, or less, of the members are real Jews. At a careful guess, there are 1,500 spread across some 30 to 33 congregations. But God never looks at numbers. We know that there were only 120 in the Upper Room, and if we had but a bit of their zeal great things would happen.

Before 1970, many Jews led a double life. Only their close

family and the people in the congregation knew that they were believers—they kept it hidden from those around them.

When we came here twenty-nine years ago, there were almost no Jewish believers who were born here. Every one was an immigrant. We had an underground complex, which was brought about due to the fact that there were hardly any Hebrew-speaking congregations. One of the first meetings that we visited in 1963 was made up of thirty people who spoke seven different languages! A youth group had started, but many young people couldn't survive the peer pressure at school or in the army.

Then there was the problem of the songs we sang. Most of our songs were translated from old Protestant Christian hymnals. So we had to grow and begin to compose our own songs.

In September 1969 the first really autonomous and non-denominational congregation was formed in Israel. Since then, many have followed. We have begun to hold youth camps for the second and third generation believers.

We now have some 200 new Hebrew songs with both music and words, and in 1989 we held the first Messianic Jewish conference of the renewed Israeli Messianic Jewish Alliance. We have had campaigns to evangelise in the streets and on the beaches, especially in Haifa and Tel Aviv. In Jerusalem it has been more difficult.

Led by the Holy Spirit, we have to create something authentically Jewish and Messianic at the same time. God has brought us into a situation where we can't just use old ways. Methods of evangelising which are used all over the world don't work here. Methods to help congregations grow which are successful elsewhere may be of no use here.

God will protect us from again becoming a sect isolated from the rest of Israel. The Messianic Jewish movement has been born of God, and can only come to full fruition through God's grace and Spirit. God has set this in motion, and only he knows where it will lead.

6
Eli, the Sabra

I met Eli Ken (thirty-three) at Qumran in the Judean desert. This is a very special place for Eli because the kibbutz Beit Ha Arava, a little to the north of the Dead Sea, was jointly founded by his father. This kibbutz was given to Jordan by the division of the land in 1948.

It was busy in Qumran. I was surrounded by thousands of Christians who had come to Jerusalem from around the world to celebrate the Feast of Tabernacles.

There comes a day, says Zechariah 14:16, that all the nations shall travel to Jerusalem to celebrate this feast before God. I heard all sorts of languages around me, and then suddenly—Dutch. Riki, a spontaneous young blonde lady, came rushing up to me calling, 'Ben, have you found Eli yet? You have to talk to him. He is a Messianic Jew who came to Holland and met Christians there. He's playing the high priest in the dance group.'

I told her that I wanted very much to meet him and straight away Riki disappeared into the crowd to find him for me. The people were standing in long queues in front of the tables, where they could collect a paper plate on which was fruit and a chicken leg. Just as God 'prepared a table in the desert' for the children of Israel, so 4,000 people were given something to eat here. Riki held on to my sleeve and pulled me along with her, and then I found myself standing opposite a young man with a black beard and laughing eyes, Eli, who said 'good evening' to me in Dutch.

I told him that I was interested in his story, and we made an appointment to meet each other on the terrace of the YMCA after the Jerusalem march. 'But first I would like to take a photo of you, Eli, because when we next meet it will be dark.' So I photographed Eli in Qumran.

When the sun goes down behind the high wall of rock the heat becomes bearable and I began to look around me. There were all those thousands of people from sixty countries, and a big silver moon that slowly rose above the mountains where Moses saw the Promised Land for the first time. The silvery light of the moon was reflected in the Dead Sea. Here Nature comes to rest and creation sings a song of worship to God.

In the meantime, a group of musicians and singers had taken their place on the podium. They sang, '*Baruch Hashem Adonai*,' and more and more people from the crowd joined in. Then a dance group appeared on a separate podium, praising God with their colourful clothes, gracious movements, and radiant faces.

The end of the feast approached, and all eyes were directed upwards. High above the rocks torches were burning; together they formed a large menorah.

And very high on the furthest spur, the floodlight lit up an Israeli flag that slowly fluttered in the sultry evening wind. Next to the famous white flag with blue stripes and Magen David I saw the Dutch red, white and blue flag flapping. I was moved.

I was born in the north of Israel, in the *moshava* Karkur, a small farming community with 3,000 inhabitants. Everyone lives independently in a *moshava* and works his piece of land as he wants. This is contrary to a *moshav*, which differs structurally. There you are not so free and everything is more organised. There you belong to a particular co-operative. We lived independently and could also work outside of the *moshava* if we wanted to; we did not have to commit ourselves to farming.

My father was born in Dortmund in Germany. He lost his father when he was still a baby. My father's mother was a rich woman, who, in her own words, 'didn't want to live in the desert' and therefore didn't emigrate to Israel with her son. She was killed by the Nazis during the war. That made my father bitter. Not straight away, but it came out later.

My father came to Israel in 1938. He was one of the founders of the kibbutz Beit Har Ava in the vicinity of Qumran. When the land was divided in 1948, the kibbutz was given to the Jordanians and my father moved to Tel Aviv. My mother is a *sabra*. She was born in Petah Tikva. Her father came from Jerusalem and her mother from Hebron. Her mother's family lived in Israel for ten generations, which is very unusual. We have deep roots here in the land, from long before Israel became a state.

A few days before I was born my father had a nervous breakdown and could no longer take care of his family. He still couldn't come to terms with the death of his father and mother and had to be taken into a psychiatric hospital, where he still is today. I grew up, therefore, in a family with only a mother.

When I was eighteen, I had to do military service just like every other Israeli. I left the familiar surroundings of my village and ended up in a totally different world. I didn't like the military atmosphere and was glad when I could leave after three and a half years.

I went to live in Jerusalem with my girlfriend, but that didn't work out very well. We thought so differently about all sorts of things. My girlfriend thought that I should go and study at the university, but I wanted to investigate everything myself. We split up.

I left my girlfriend behind in our flat and went to live in another part of Jerusalem. I took all sorts of odd jobs, even if they didn't suit me.

One day I got a job in the absorption centre in Jerusalem. That is a centre where all newly arrived immigrants get temporary accommodation. The work suited me. I helped immigrants who knew nothing of the outlook or the language in our country.

In the absorption centre I met a woman from South America. She couldn't prove that she was a Jew and her case had to be looked into first, before she could be accepted.

During that time the war in Lebanon broke out. Three times I had to go deep into Lebanon. Every day there were some more dead soldiers to mourn for. Besides that, we had an economic crisis, with inflation reaching 1,000 per cent.

It was a time full of tension with very little prospect of improvement. I felt under so much pressure through this that I decided to leave the country for a while. I didn't know for how long.

At first I lived in Spain for seven months. But when I heard that our army had pulled out of Lebanon and that everything was getting back to normal, I went back to Israel.

I found work as a salesman among the Arabs in Judea and Samaria, and could get along very well with the Arabs. I got in touch with my South American girlfriend and her three children and we began to work together. We worked in the occupied areas and made many friends. Some were

Christians, others Muslims, but it didn't make any difference to us, we could get on with them all very well. That is until the conversation turned to religion or politics, causing the discussion to flag. Nowadays they would not accept me as they used to because of the *Intifada*. Once that started, the shops were closed and the tension rose. We couldn't do any more business; there was no more money to be made.

My girlfriend found work in a hospital. We started living together and the fact that we gave her three children such a bad example still hurts me.

In the hospital my girlfriend became aquainted with an Arab believer from Nazareth. She gave her a Spanish New Testament with the Hebrew text alongside the Spanish. It was a little green book. I visited her once at the hospital and saw that little green book lying there. Never in my life had I opened a New Testament. We had once had neighbours from the United States who called themselves Messianic Jews, but I didn't know what that meant then. They had invited us over once and spoke about the Holy Land and the life of Yeshua. They had also wanted to give me a New Testament, but I wouldn't accept it at the time.

Now this book had come my way again and something touched my heart so that I suddenly wanted to know what was in it. I was taking a course in hotel reception work and therefore had to know about Judaism, Christianity and Islam. We studied tourism in general, and especially in Israel. We were expected to be able to give extra information about the Holy Land and the various religions to anyone who came to the reception desk.

One teacher was a guide himself and he took us into the old city with him. He took us past a mosque and told us about Islam. But he didn't add, 'Watch out for Islam,' or, 'Islam is dangerous.' However, when this guide took us to the Church of the Holy Sepulchre and explained every step of the way to the cross to us, he did warn us, 'Don't believe it, it's not for you, it is dangerous.' That made me very curious. Why did he say this only about Christianity?

I didn't have any problem with Judaism. I didn't have a religious background, but the Jewish tradition was known at home, although I didn't wear a *kippah* or go to the synagogue. I hardly ever read the *Siddur*. I didn't think it necessary to parade my faith; that was something deep in you which you had to decide about yourself.

But now I began to have doubts about what the guide had said about Christianity. Maybe what he had said in the church in the old city wasn't all true. I had to investigate for myself. The following day I went to the old city again and walked to the Church of the Holy Sepulchre and took an Arab guide with me. I asked him, 'Would you take me round?' He led me round and at every step he said exactly the same things that my Jewish guide had said, except for his warning, 'Don't believe it,' or 'Be careful.'

And now that little green book lay waiting for me in the hospital where my girlfriend worked. I opened it at Matthew 1:1 and began to read. When I read about Yeshua, how his life began and how he grew up, I recognised a longing in myself to come into contact with his personality.

I didn't see him as the Son of God, but as a person. He had been born of a mother just like any other person. I just couldn't believe that Mary had been a virgin.

Now I also discovered a difference between what my guide had said and what the New Testament taught, namely the date upon which Yeshua was born. He had said that Herod the Great had died before Yeshua was born. But in Matthew it was written that Yeshua went to Egypt and lived there for a few years until Herod had died.

I wanted to lay that before my guide. So the following day I took the New Testament with me to the lesson and opened it in front of my guide's eyes and the whole class. Everyone was shocked! I didn't think that I'd done anything wrong. We had studied material based on Josephus Flavius' book, which gave a detailed description from the same period, so why not read the New Testament alongside it?

My guide was horrified and didn't even want to touch the New Testament, so I read aloud the piece that dealt with the birth of Christ myself. The guide didn't want to know about it. 'They can write what they want, it isn't of interest to me.' I thought, 'He says that he bases everything on facts and knowledge, but he denies them when they don't come in handy.' So I closed the little book and put it back in my bag. The lesson continued without discussion.

I loved my country—it was my only fatherland on earth—but I wanted to distance myself from everything and study new things. I said to my girlfriend, 'We're going to Norway to find work in the fish industry, earn a lot of money and then start a small hotel in Spain.' That was one of my reasons for doing a hotel reception course.

We took a KLM flight from Tel Aviv to Amsterdam to catch the train to Norway from there. We arrived in Amsterdam just before the weekend and realised that we would spend the *Shabbat* somewhere on the journey if we took the train at once. So we found a place to sleep in a hostel and took a look around.

For the first time we were struck by the open-mindedness of the Dutch. We thought, 'We've landed in a totally different world.' In some respects that's very negative, and again in others positive.

For example, we saw how drugs were being used on the street. Drugs were offered to us openly, with the police watching but doing nothing about it.

We stayed in Amsterdam for three days and compared everything we saw with life in the Middle East. For instance, when we went to a travel agent to arrange our train journey to Norway, the assistant who helped us was so nice to us. She gave us her full attention. We took everything in.

I stood by a bus stop and saw that the bus stopped very close to the pavement, so that the people could get in easily.

That caught my attention, just like thousands of other details.

Then we got on the Northern Express and travelled by train through Germany, Denmark, Sweden and Norway.

When we reached the German border our passports were checked. The German customs officer stepped into our compartment, didn't say anything—no 'good evening' or the like—but just stuck out his hand. His uniform was green, whereas the Dutch have blue uniforms just like we have in Israel. It gave us an uncomfortable feeling.

In Denmark the people were very nice to us. They asked us what we were going to do, and so on. In Sweden it was a little more difficult. But in Norway we again felt real freedom. Even crossing the border was nothing. We passed through the border without any control. Here a Swedish flag and then a Norwegian one—and that's all. You come into another world.

I looked for work for a week. But there wasn't any work available. The people told us the sea had been over fished and that the fishing industry wasn't doing too well. And life in Norway is very expensive. We saw our savings dwindle before our very eyes. We said to each other, 'If we go on like this we'll be broke before long.'

Before it got that far, we thought it better to return to Holland to see if we could find work there. What's more, it is less cold in Holland and the people live more on the street there than in Scandinavia.

So we took the train back to Amsterdam. Luckily we met someone from South America who took us into his home, so we didn't need to live in a hostel any more. And . . . I found work in a fish factory. It was heavy work, but one way or another we were able to stay in Holland for quite a long time.

The tension between my girlfriend and the two children that we had taken with us and myself—one of her children had stayed behind in Israel with the grandmother—increased. The journey to the north of Europe had changed us both a lot. Our relationship had altered as a result. I thought, 'Now I have to think of myself, which means we have to split up.'

Before that happened, we made a trip together to a village in Overijssel, a village built along a canal. On a Sunday morning we were walking along by a row of houses and my girlfriend was crying. Then we heard the sound of singing. To my ears it was as if I was being called. I knew nothing about church services. I had been in many churches, but never during a service. I asked my girlfriend, 'Do you hear that singing too?' She said, 'Yes.'

We could see where it was coming from—a little white building. It seemed too small to really be a church. We walked up to it and pushed the door open. The little building was full and the church service had already begun.

The minister, who stood at the front, was shocked when we came in, because no one ever came in during the middle of the service. I thought, 'Perhaps he can see from the colour of my skin that I'm not from here, and forgive my behaviour.'

There was a friendly old lady in the back row who beckoned to us and gave us each a little black book. I found that typical Dutch individualism. With her finger she pointed to each song as it was sung. 'Psalms and Hymns' it said on the little book.

I didn't understand any Dutch. But when I looked through the little book, I saw familiar words—'Psalms of King David'—and that made me feel more at home. It was special to hear these Dutch village people singing about David, Jerusalem and Israel.

After the service was over we were walking back along the canal when a car drew up beside us. It was the minister from the Christian Reformed Church that we had just visited. He asked us where we had come from and was surprised to hear that we came from Jerusalem. He said that we were always welcome in his church.

I went along more often, but my girlfriend didn't want to go with me regularly. People from the church picked me up by car on Sundays and took me to the church.

I wanted to learn the language of the man in the street. I could speak English with people who had studied, but I wanted to converse with ordinary Dutch people. So I went to the church and began to learn Dutch.

Every Sunday I understood more of the sermon. I watched the minister's mouth intently and tried to say some words just like he did. And after a few weeks I could already join in a conversation using a few words.

Once I asked the minister a question: 'Why do you read the Ten Commandments every Sunday, and one of the commandments is that we should keep the day of *Shabbat*, but you keep the Sunday?' He explained to me that people in the church kept strictly to certain rules, and didn't move away from them. I understood that, but still asked questions again and again. Also, we could not take part in the Communion. I discovered that you're not supposed to ask questions, even if you've spent all your life in the church, otherwise you can't take Communion. But they were very kind to us and made us feel at home, and I'm very thankful for that. God will bless them for it.

We moved to South Holland and from Overijssel they phoned the local church so that someone could look us up. It was very nice that someone cared about us. The Dutch are friendly people.

I also went to church every Sunday in the new place. Never in my life had I been so taken up with religion. I didn't believe that Yeshua was the Son of God, but I did find it very strange that all these people went to church faithfully every Sunday to hear about Yeshua, who was a Jew.

The tension between my girlfriend and myself reached a

climax and we split up. My girlfriend and her children later went back to Israel, and I travelled another 200 kilometres to south Limburg.

I went to the church again there. But it was a different sort of church, with a large cross on top of it. When I went in, I saw a statue and also a large cross on the wall. I couldn't cope with that very well.

It was nearing *Rosh Hashanah* and I discovered that there was a synagogue in Maastricht. I went there, but I didn't feel spiritually at home. The rabbi was rather nervous. He ran back and forth because there weren't enough books for all those present. I thought, 'This is no place for me.'

But I didn't feel at home in the church either, especially not with that large cross on the wall. So I stayed at home for a few weeks. I only went out to do some shopping. I studied the Dutch dictionary and began to speak much better Dutch. But I wanted to see people and suffered from loneliness.

So I began to write letters to my mother in Israel. I told her about my struggle, that I didn't fancy being a soldier on patrol in Judea and Samaria, where I used to sell for a living. I might meet friends with whom I'd done business earlier, and I would be in uniform and carrying a weapon. I said, 'The people in these northern countries also love their country, just like me, but they are open enough to accept me as a Jew, even though they are Christians. That's how we should live together with the Arabs.' But today the Arabs are showing a very different face. I cannot freely travel in their villages as before.

At home alone on the *Shabbat*, I lit the candles and read my Bible. I began to believe in that word more and more. It was the truth. It was given to me by God.

Then *Pesach* came, the feast to celebrate the liberation of the Jews from Egypt and all other countries. I realised that it was necessary for me to go home, even though I wasn't a slave like the Jews in Egypt. But I didn't want to travel to Israel too quickly, so I took the bus to Greece first. I travelled through Germany again, and again felt the change in atmosphere, just like the first time.

After that I went through Yugoslavia and from there to Greece. There I found a ship which would leave for Haifa five days later. In the meantime I hung around. I didn't feel like seeing all the sights in Greece because this spiritual battle was going on inside me. I didn't know how best to deal with everything I had experienced.

On the day of departure I saw a little man with a somewhat dark face and black hair by the entrance to the harbour. I asked him in English, 'Where do you come from?'

He answered in broken English, 'I come from Peru in South America.'

I told him that he could talk to me in Spanish. Through my work in the absorption centre, and the years that I'd lived with my South American girlfriend, I had learned to speak Spanish well.

He was glad that he had met someone who could speak his language and asked where I was going. When he heard that I was taking the boat to Haifa, he was even happier, because he was booked on that one too; now he could speak in Spanish for the entire journey.

On the voyage he asked me a lot about Israel and I taught him a song in Hebrew, '*Kol haolam kulo gesher tsar meod*'. When we arrived in Haifa three days later, he could sing the song well.

He was on his way to a church in Jerusalem. I knew every church in Jerusalem and therefore asked him which church he was going to. But he only had a telephone number. I thought, 'That's a bit risky. What if the number isn't right? Then you're lost,' because he didn't have the name of a single person to contact.

We travelled together to Jerusalem and he came to my home with me to see my mother. We had a meal together

and afterwards I said, 'Try calling. See if anyone answers
on that telephone number.' He telephoned and got the South
American Congregation on the line, who straight away
invited him to come to them. He thanked me and left. But
I made a note of the number for contact later. I tried to find
a job but that was difficult. In those days there were many
unemployed in Israel.

Then came the terrorist attack on bus 405 on the road
from Tel Aviv to Jerusalem. Several people died in the attack
and there were many wounded. I thought, 'There are
Spanish tourists among them, I'll go and visit them in the
hospital.'

I went to the Hadassah hospital and found a Spanish girl
from Catalonia. I spoke to her and she asked if I would
come back again.

Just at that time my friend from Peru phoned me, and
when I told him about the Spanish-speaking girl, his pastor,
Jaime Buertas, asked if he could come to the hospital with
me. We arranged that we would meet at the entrance to the
hospital at nine o'clock.

When I arrived, he looked at me and said, 'You have a
lot of light in your face, do you know that?' We visited the
girl, and when we were saying goodbye to her, Jaime said,
'We'll pray as well.' That wasn't new for me, because I was
used to people saying grace before eating in Holland.

We walked to the bus together. At that period I was still
full of questions about God and the New Testament. I also
had a Bible in my bag. For one reason or another I trusted
Jaime. In the bus I opened my Bible and asked him a few
questions, and he gave me very wise answers. He said, 'Let's
talk about Immanuel,' and he gave me many passages of
Scripture which proved that Mashiach had already come,
long ago.

He let me read about the suffering Immanuel. He said
that he was a manifestation of God. I knew exactly what
he was talking about due to my study of the New

Testament, but I didn't tell him that. While we were riding through Jerusalem on the bus, Jaime Buertas taught me about Immanuel.

But I still had so many questions. All sorts of pieces of the puzzle, from what I'd heard or maybe believed myself, had to be put together. Jaime gave me these passages from the Bible and I began to have a much clearer picture.

'Come to us for lunch,' he invited.

I said, 'All right.'

We changed buses for Neve Ja'acov, where he lived. There we talked for three hours. I was hungry and thirsty to know more about God.

At a specific moment he asked me, 'Do you believe that Immanuel in the Old Testament is the same as Yeshua in the New Testament and that he is also your Redeemer?'

I quickly repeated this same question to myself.

'Eli, do you believe that he is your Saviour?'

In my mind I heard the question echo and said to myself, 'Eli, it is so clear, you can't say no.'

After what seemed a long time, I said very definitely, 'Yes!'

When I said that, everyone in the room began to dance. I felt a great joy come over me. Everyone who was present felt the same joy.

I believe that God had let me learn Spanish in order to allow me hear the message in Spanish. Even though I had lived in sin when I learned Spanish, God had brought good from the bad. He always does that. God used the Spanish language and the love of the Christians to open my heart to Yeshua. So Jaime Buertas became my personal pastor. He still is today.

I looked for a place where I could go and worship God. One day I was walking through Narkis Street in the centre of Jerusalem and there I saw a man who looked exactly like someone I had met in South Holland. I thought, 'Why shouldn't I speak to this man?' I turned around and said, 'You look exactly like someone I met in Holland.'

He told me that his forefathers had come from Holland, but that he had never been there himself. I also asked what he did and he told me that he was an elder in the Baptist church. But he didn't invite me to come to Baptist House. So I asked him myself, 'May I come to the church too?'

He said, 'Yes, you are welcome every *Shabbat* at 10.30 am.'

I went there and I am still attending that church today. I sometimes do the Hebrew reading, and organise transport for people to the church because there is no public transport on the *Shabbat*.

I feel very involved in the spiritual life in Jerusalem. My vision is to open a large house in Jerusalem where people from all nationalities and religions will be welcome—a sort of hostel. I know what it means to live alone in a foreign city and want to create a warm place, where people feel welcome.

I am still single. Only the Lord can give me the right wife. Many young people, also believers, are too hasty in finding a partner and end up with all sorts of problems. I wait for God's time.

That goes for the Messianic Jewish believers too. We also must grow at the pace that God wants for us. For us it is slower than for the believers from the nations. We must always go back to the basic question, 'How can we reconcile the image of God and that of Yeshua?' Lately I have seen more Orthodox Jews looking forward to the coming of Mashiach. A few think that there's a real possibility that Yeshua is the Meshiach. They can't say this out loud, but the thought is there among them.

Even more Jews will come to faith in the future. This is my hope and prayer.

7
Michael, the Yeshiva *student*

I met Michael Guberman (twenty-five) for the first time during the Hebrew-language service in Christ Church in the old city. You go through the Jaffa Gate, past the Citadel, David's Tower, and then, on the left, you see a coffee shop, a bookshop and the gate to a hostel. Christ Church is behind there.

This church has had a special relationship with the Jews since 1849. There are Jewish symbols and Hebrew letters incorporated in the stained-glass windows, the Communion table and on a large plaque on the back wall.

The founders of the church took Romans 1:16 seriously, where it says, 'I am not ashamed of the gospel, because it is the power of God for the salvation of everyone who believes: first for the Jew, then for the Gentile.' These founders already saw that God would bring the Jewish people back to their land, even in the time of the Turks.

On Sabbath afternoons, many Messianic Jews come together here to praise God and to hear his word.

Michael translated Rufen Berger's sermon for the English-speaking listeners. Beatrice, his fiancée, sat next to him and during the singing they kept giving each other loving glances, now and then whispering something in each other's ear. It is difficult to imagine that this is the same young man who studied at the *Yeshiva* dressed in a black suit.

I was born in New York. When I was ten years old, we moved to the south of the United States, to Virginia.

My father and mother are Jews, but we didn't observe our religious obligations as we should have. At *Chanukah* we lit the candles, and we also kept a few of the other feast days—a special meal with *Pesach*, and so on. Actually, my Jewish upbringing consisted primarily of the rules: 'Be proud that you are a Jew, remember your family that was killed in the holocaust, never marry a Gentile and don't get caught up with the New Testament and Jesus. Because the Christians always try to rob us of our Jewish identity one way or another.'

Absolutely no Jews lived in the city that we ended up in. In fact, I grew up without any idea of what my religion contained. Most Jewish children still get some form of religious education when they are being made ready for their *Bar Mitzvah*, but I didn't. My childhood was not always easy for there was a lot of tension in my home. I had a hunger for spiritual things which wasn't being satisfied. Therefore, I often went into the countryside alone.

We lived in Virginia in a land with a lot of natural beauty. I didn't have many friends, so I spent a lot of time alone in the woods and in the open fields. I felt something of God's presence in the countryside. I didn't understand that then, but if I now look back, I know that there was something special surrounding me.

I had a good friend who began to believe in Jesus. He wasn't a Jew. The area where we lived was called the 'Bible belt', because there are so many churches and believers there. This friend of mine was poor. The house where he and his fifteen brothers and sisters lived was just a stable, without running water or electricity.

He became really fired-up for the Lord and also began to speak to me about his faith. I thought, 'You're a poor boy, you have nothing in this world, so it's good for you.' But I also saw the tremendous change in his life. That made a deep impression on me. On top of that, he looked very happy. As a fourteen-year-old I was very unhappy and deep in my heart I longed for the same things he had: joy and hope.

My friend challenged me to read the New Testament. At first I said, 'No, I can't. That's forbidden for me as a Jew. It may be all right for you, but not for me.' I had never read the Bible, not even the Old Testament.

My friend said, 'That's not right. You, as an intellectual, read all sorts of difficult books and you won't even open the New Testament. How can you judge something that you haven't even read? You're probably afraid of what you're going to discover.'

He'd got me with that; so I went to the section where the Bibles were in the school library. That was a forbidden area for me, somewhere I didn't even dare walk. I walked backwards and forwards up the aisle several times. When I was convinced that no one could see, I picked up a Bible, had it checked out, and took it home hidden under my coat. My mother must not be allowed to see what I was doing.

I went to my room and opened the New Testament. I had thought that I would read about how bad the Jews are and that they had murdered Jesus and are cursed. Perhaps there would also be nice things in it, like 'turn the other cheek'. But whatever was good in it would have to come from the Old Testament. I hadn't thought that I would find anything in it which would speak to me in a personal way.

I opened the New Testament and was amazed. I read a piece from Matthew 5, the account of the Sermon on the Mount. I read something like, 'Blessed are you, when you

have no father or mother, because the Lord is your father
and mother.' It affected me so deeply that my mouth fell
open in astonishment. I'd absolutely not expected to find
anything like that. It touched me deeply and I began to cry.
In those days I felt especially lonely, because there wasn't a
lot of warmth in our family. That's why it affected me so.

I've tried very often since then to find that text again,
but the strange thing is that it doesn't say that. It says,
'Blessed are you for . . . this and for that,' but there are no
special promises of a blessing for the orphans.

Years went by before I discovered that God's word is
living. It isn't a traditional piece of literature, but something
through which the Holy Spirit can speak to us in a personal
way. God gave me precisely that word which I needed. I
cried and suddenly realised that God really exists. I was so
happy that God was real and was close by and that he was
there for me, when I didn't have anyone else in the world.

I was placed in a children's home and I went to a Baptist
church. Unfortunately there were a lot of problems in the
church. I didn't know anything about Christianity and the
church, and that there are differences between one church
and another. Up to a certain point I accepted the Lord. But
my Jewishness still worried me somewhat. In this church
they preached replacement theology—that the church has
come in the place of Israel.

They told me that I was the first Jew to come through
the church door. 'Look what we have here,' they said. 'We
have a Jew in the church.' But to me they said, 'You are
now a Christian and not a Jew any more and you must be
happy, because God has set you free from the curse of your
forefathers.' In those days I was so open-minded that I
accepted that! I thought, 'The New Testament has done
something so wonderful for me, I want to go on with this.'

But I discovered something else in this church: racism. I
noticed that no black people came to this church. When I
asked why that was, I got only vague answers. Because I

had been a victim of racism as a Jewish boy, I couldn't accept their reacting in this way in this church.

As a child I was once beaten for being Jewish. On one occasion the windows in our house were smashed and slogans were painted on our walls. People had let us know that we were not welcome, because we were Jewish and different from the rest.

I had always had the feeling that there were two things about me that weren't good: that I came from New York and that I was a Jew. My parents, especially, suffered through this; they could never feel totally at home there. As a child, the transition was somewhat easier for me. But here in this church I came up against it again: you are a Jew, you don't fit in. When we read the Old Testament stories in Sunday school, the teachers regularly turned to me with the question: 'Have I said it right?' They thought that I knew the Old Testament inside out. But it gave me the feeling that I was different from the others.

I thought, 'God exists and he is interested in me, but I don't know who he is. I have to study my own religion.' But there were no Jews in my area, so I didn't do too well in getting more information. I left the church and tried to forget my experience of Christianity.

When I had finished high school, war between Israel and Lebanon broke out and I wanted to go to Israel to fight in the army. I thought, 'This is my chance to discover the purpose of my life, to live among my own people and to get to know God better.' I didn't actually know much about Israel, although I had had a desire to go to Israel since childhood.

I came here and straight away became an Israeli citizen and enlisted in the army. I still didn't know any Hebrew and went into the army unprepared. It was a strange culture.

The war in Lebanon came to an end and the other soldiers said to me, 'You're crazy to leave America to come here. We're all trying to get out of the country and you come

here.' I realised that I had made a great mistake in joining
the army and I felt lonelier than ever. But I still wanted to
find my roots. There were Orthodox boys in the army and
I began to get interested in what they told me about their
faith.

After two years I left the army and visited a friend who
studied at the *Yeshiva* at Beney Brak near Tel Aviv. The
Yeshiva seemed almost as big as a city. It was a *Yeshiva*
where people without an Orthodox background could also
study. They taught you from the very first principles.

I only went there to study for two weeks and after that
to move on again. I declared immediately upon my arrival,
'I'm not staying here, I'm only coming for two weeks and
I won't become Orthodox.' That resulted in all the students
and rabbis seeing it as their personal mission to convince
me that I should become Orthodox. They put a lot of
pressure on me in the form of, 'This is a matter of truth
and non-truth, the most important thing in your life. How
can you give it just two weeks of your life?' Or, 'If you're
really honest, give yourself at least a month here.'

I had a ticket to fly back to the United States, so I said,
'I have to go back in two weeks, otherwise my ticket
expires.' They said, 'Change your ticket then.' So I extended
it by a month and began to study.

Then they said, 'If you let your ticket expire and stay a
year, we'll provide a new ticket.' I thought that was all right,
and they reckoned, 'If we have him here for a year, he'll
have become Orthodox and certainly won't want to leave
any more.'

The truth is, I could never forget the precious experience
I had had with God. I knew something was missing in my
life and I would never be at peace with myself if I didn't
find it. I had to sort myself out with God and in one way
or another start to live for him otherwise I would never be
happy.

Actually, I wanted to accept the Orthodox lifestyle, if

that could reinforce my Jewish identity. I threw myself into it with heart and soul. I gave everything that I had to give to that study. I became very Orthodox and enjoyed my studies. I found the *Talmud* and the rabbinical writings a challenge. They stimulated my intellect and I had a certain aptitude for understanding them.

The study was satisfying and the rabbis were very encouraging. That heightened my pride again. I caught up with my friend who had gone to the *Yeshiva* a year earlier, and that also made me feel proud. The rabbis gave me all sorts of honours, which pleased me. I was an especially serious student and devoted all my energies to studying. I studied day and night to the point of exhaustion. But still I had no peace.

There were things in the *Talmud* that I couldn't believe. The purity and simplicity of the Bible had got lost. The Bible is open for everyone. Each person can understand it and believe in God. There are no rules in it so complicated that it takes a lifetime of study to be able to understand their meaning.

But I suppressed these inconsistencies by studying. I wanted so much for Orthodoxy to have the answer. So the unhappier I became, the more I studied. Some people leave the *Yeshiva* if they have doubts in their heart which come to the fore. Others do the opposite: they become so fanatical that they drown the doubts with their study.

I became more and more extremely Orthodox. I even dressed the part, with black clothes and a black hat. I followed the Lithuanian tradition which emphasises scholastic ability, as opposed to the Chassidic movement which emphasises ethical and emotional experiences.

It became a vicious circle. I became more and more involved; that made it harder, and through that I became even more involved.

I was nearing the point of collapse. I slept in the study hall on a bench and was the first to pray again in the morning. I began at four o'clock in the morning, prayed and studied until seven o'clock, took a quick breakfast and studied the whole day through until deep into the night.

I was given a lot of praise and recognition, but it didn't satisfy me. This went on for three and a half years. Then I received a visit. My parents came over from the United States. I had then reached the peak of my academic achievement and was honoured with the title 'rabbi', the proof that I had reached a certain level in my study.

I was proud of it, but at the same time my fanatical striving came to an end. I had driven myself on, torturing myself with the idea, 'It is like putting a small fortune in the bank. You mustn't ask any questions now, because later on you will get the interest from it.'

Now that I was at the point of leaving the *Yeshiva*, the rabbis were encouraging me to marry, because I would soon be a teacher myself.

By this time I should have been thankful and satisfied, but I wasn't. I should have had certainty, but I was full of questions. It was through that that I lost my motivation. I thought of my friend in Virginia. He had had peace and joy when he became a Christian, but I was in a spiritual prison. I wanted to do everything I could to have this peace for myself too.

And so from within the *Yeshiva* I began secretly seeking contact with Messianic Jews. I knew that they existed, because the Orthodox Jews persecuted them. They wanted me to take part in an anti-missions organisation which opposed the Messianic Jews. But I never joined in, because I knew in my heart that these were the ones who had got it right.

Through the information which I obtained from this organisation, I began to make contact with the Messianic Jews. I visited a bookshop and bought a New Testament and a couple of other Christian books and began to read them in secret. Gradually Jesus became more and more important to me.

The rabbis thought that things were going wrong for me because I wasn't married. So they began pressurising me to marry. The rabbi would seek out a woman for you and arrange a meeting. They thought that the daughter of a well-known rabbi would be suitable for me.

A place and time had been arranged so that we could meet each other for the first time. My rabbi and her rabbi and her father were present and we spoke about all kinds of subjects and tried to find out if we were compatible.

If you are satisfied with the other person, you let your own rabbi know that afterwards and he then speaks with her rabbi and a second meeting follows. And if you don't like the other person, the contact is broken and then they come with a new candidate. If it all goes well, a speedy engagement and a wedding follow.

I had no desire to marry this woman, because it would mean being bogged down in Orthodoxy for the rest of my life. I knew that it was impossible to believe in Jesus and be Orthodox. That's something like being handed the key and still staying in your cell. We talked about our interests, our backgrounds, where we would like to live, and so on. We did feel attracted to one another. But I knew that I had to break it off, even though it would be very difficult.

My life fell apart. I became very depressed and lost all interest in my study. The *Yeshiva* didn't understand what was the matter with me. They decided, 'Let's send him to another school, the *Yeshiva* in Jerusalem. Perhaps the change of scenery will do him good.'

I thought that was fine, because I knew that there were more believers in Jerusalem than in Beney Brak. Perhaps I could get in touch with them, then I could ask for advice about how to break away. I didn't have enough spiritual energy to break loose myself.

When I was in Jerusalem, I went to the Garden Tomb,

the garden by Jesus' empty grave, to pray and to seek the
Lord. I prayed, 'Lord, now you must show me where I
should go, and what I should do, because I'm at my wits'
end. I can't go on like this.' After that I felt calmer.

I left the Garden Tomb and walked through the old city,
to catch the bus near the Jaffa Gate. And there by the Jaffa
Gate I saw the church: Christ Church. Of course I'd been
along that way often, because the church was on the way
to the Jewish quarter of the old city. But I had never paid
much attention to it, even though I thought it was a bit
strange: a church in the Arab quarter.

A sign on the fence said, 'The oldest Anglican church in
the Middle East,' but I had never had any interest in
churches. I thought they were intimidating and big and I
knew that Jews weren't liked in them. Cathedrals didn't do
anything for me either. I always went out of my way to
avoid them. But now I was really drawn to it.

I went in. Someone was working there as a receptionist,
an Israeli girl from a kibbutz. She was a believer. I spoke
to her. At first I was surprised to find an Israeli girl in an
Arab district and not only that, but one who believed in
Yeshua! I felt that she was a really upright believer and I
told her what was troubling me. She introduced me to other
people in Christ Church.

I also met a young man whom I knew from my time in
the army. When I was on leave, I had gone to his apparte-
ment in Haifa. He was married to a woman who also
believed in Yeshua. It was just one surprise after another. He
recognised me and said, 'If you want to leave the *Yeshiva*,
you can stay with us.' I felt very flattered, but rejected the
idea because I didn't want to impose on their family. But
I said that I would think about it and left, to go back to the
Yeshiva again.

I was amazed at what I had discovered. I had met believers
and people who were prepared to share their lives with me.

A couple of days later I came back to my room in the

Yeshiva and found it in chaos. Everything had been turned upside down. Someone had apparently seen that I had gone into Christ Church. They accused me of making illicit contacts. They had found Christian literature in my room.

When I came in, they said, 'Now we understand what your problem is.' And, 'Normally we show someone who does these things the door. But we've known you for years and know how devoted you were. Perhaps because the contact with this woman concerning a possible marriage hasn't worked out you are depressed and have gone to the wrong place to find the answers. We can't imagine that you believe any of that. You were only looking, so we're going to give you another chance and try to help you. We shall give you money and do everything we can to help you. But on one condition: you have to renounce Jesus and everything connected with him; burn these books, including the Bible. We give you ten minutes in which to do it.'

It was in the middle of the night and it was pouring with rain. The past half year, during which I had lived as a secret believer in the *Yeshiva*, passed through my thoughts. All this time I had been tossed back and forth and now everything had come to a head. I had to choose.

I threw a few items of clothing into a bag and went out of the door, into the rain. All my possessions remained behind. I thought, 'I'll collect them some other time.' But that has never happened, I have never been back. I had felt like a hypocrite all the time that I was a believer in the *Yeshiva* and that made me feel guilty.

Was it worth while to be a believer?

When I was out on the streets in Jerusalem, in the middle of the night, I thought about the offer from that couple to come and live with them. I took the bus and knocked on their door and they received me as a brother.

During the months that I stayed with them, the Lord began to heal the pain in my heart—the pain of rejection. I had to develop my own personality and learn to be myself.

The Hebrew-speaking congregation in Christ Church was just beginning to develop, and I grew with it.

The leaders have a large house where they would take in young believers and help them grow in the Lord. I lived there for two years.

Now I have my own flat here in Jerusalem, and I'm very happy there. I have lived in the army, in the *Yeshiva* and with other Christians, now I finally have a place of my own. I have a job in the bookshop at Christ Church and in Beatrice I have found my future wife.

My Orthodox friends ignore me. Some have tried to persuade me that I should come back. But mostly they just look the other way. This is a small country so you always come across each other again.

It took me a few years to get over the feeling of guilt, leaving the *Yeshiva*. But as I became stronger I knew that I had done the right thing; as I became stronger I could forget the past better. And my faith in Jesus gives me great joy. I have had more joy and experienced more blessings than ever before in my life.

God has healed my wounds from the past, and has brought me into a deeper relationship with himself. I have also developed in my own personality. I can now look back on my moderate Jewish background at home as well as the strict Orthodox time. Now I can understand the Jews as well as the Gentiles.

Now and then I have the chance of bringing the message of Yeshua to Orthodox Jews and that makes a big impression on them, especially because of the example of my own life and also because of my knowledge of their way of life.

I am thankful to God that the dividing wall has been broken down and that his life and joy have been made available to all the peoples on earth. In our congregation Jews and Gentiles come together and we are truly one in Christ.

I believe that the future direction of my life is to proclaim his word and to build a bridge between Jews and Gentiles.

I love my country and the people here as never before. I feel at home here, but that is also because I have come 'home' to God. In this country this bridge is especially necessary, as also is one between the Jews and the Arabs.

Together with all believers in all countries we are building 'a temple of living stones' which will result in, as Paul writes, 'life from the dead' (Rom 11:15).

8
Lewis, the Seeker

Lewis Sherman told me his story in the little office behind the bookshop at Christ Church in the old city of Jerusalem. There were moments when I had to stop my cassette recorder to give him a chance to pull himself together.

In particular, the description of the vision he had had of Jesus moved him afresh.

God has shown him that he has a special love for Jerusalem. He has brought him to 'the city where God will live' (Ps 132:14), contrary to all his own plans. 'Since then,' says Lewis, 'my love for Jerusalem has only grown.'

When I had finished the interview, I walked into the Jewish district to take photos by the Wailing Wall. I didn't know it, but there, on the Temple Square, a riot had broken out.

While I walked through the narrow streets, stopping every now and then to look at little shops selling beautiful paintings or sculptures, I saw a mother trying to comfort a baby who was crying and coughing violently in its pram.

Then something pricked in my own eyes . . . tear gas.

I climbed up a small wall and looked out over the square

139

before the Wailing Wall and the Temple Mount with the golden domed mosque behind it. The square in front of the Wailing Wall was empty. Normally, during the Feast of Tabernacles, tens of thousands of Jews would be standing there to pray.

A few hours earlier, Arab youths had begun to throw stones down on the praying Jews, so that stones rained down on the square. I saw how soldiers had forced the gate, and run into the Temple Square, firing as they went, to drive out the Arab youths. In the process, twenty-one Arab youths were killed and 125 wounded, and nineteen Israelis were wounded. It was a deeply emotional experience.

The tears were running down my face, not only from the tear gas that blew across from the Temple Mount, but because I could also feel the enormous spiritual battle that rages through this place. I thought of the text, 'You will arise and have compassion on Zion, for it is time to show favour to her' (Ps 102:13). How much blood will still have to flow before this piece of 'Promised Land' can also be possessed and the Messiah can return?

I was born in 1944 in Brooklyn, New York, into a Jewish family. My Orthodox grandparents had an especially strong influence on my life. They made sure that I was brought up in the Jewish faith.

From the age of six I attended Hebrew school as well as receiving the normal education. When I was seven years old, I knew intuitively that my real life would begin only when I had found the truth. But I didn't know what that meant.

I followed all the Jewish traditions and had little contact with Gentile children. I never heard the gospel either.

My only experience of Christianity was that I was beaten up and harassed on various occasions by people who told me that we Jews had killed Jesus.

I decided, after my *Bar Mitzvah* when I was thirteen, to

investigate other religions. I tried to speak with the rabbis during religious studies about the deeper questions I had, because I found it intolerable to have to keep repeating prayers without knowing what they meant. You were expected to do this even if you didn't understand any of it. I had a deep desire to get to know the truth.

I didn't want to explore Christianity. I had had only negative experiences of it. Actually, I knew very little about Christianity. I thought, for example, that the different denominations all had different Bibles.

After my thirteenth birthday I began to get interested in philosophy, and at the same time I began my music studies. At a very young age I played the guitar professionally and so became acquainted with the world of music and entertainment.

Through that I also came into contact with drugs. In those days drug abuse was rampant throughout the music scene in New York and I fell into that pit. As the Bible says, 'Bad company destroys good behaviour.' My path went downhill and I began using an increasing variety of drugs and became addicted to them.

It was a dark time in my life, which I'd rather not think back on. In 1968 I had run out of money for my music studies at the Berkeley School of Music in Boston and I went back to New York to work as a musician for a year. I hoped to be able to save some money to go back to school and finish my studies.

But it was during the Vietnam war and from the moment that I left the school I could be called up for military service. I decided to go abroad as quickly as possible. I had friends with a Scandinavian background so I thought, 'I'll go to Sweden.' Everything I'd heard about Scandinavia was positive. I remembered Danny Kaye's film of Hans Christian Anderson's story in which 'the Pied Piper' walked around the fountain in Copenhagen. That was my idea of Scandinavia and that's what I wanted to see.

I told my parents I was leaving the United States, maybe not to return for ten years. I took my guitar and backpack and got on the plane to Copenhagen. But I stayed only a short time in Copenhagen, playing with a few other musicians—but I didn't feel at ease.

I went to visit a friend in Sweden, a forty-minute boat trip and twenty-minute train journey to the university city of Lund. There I met my Swedish wife. She was studying at the university and we started living together.

We were both seekers who didn't believe in conventional marriage. We investigated different religions and sects. I was a long way away from God in those days, but I still had that great desire for the truth.

Quite by chance I read a book by a philosopher, not a Christian, who said there was something special about the Gospels. I thought, 'Since I've investigated just about everything else, why not also read the Gospels?'

We had moved to Stockholm, the capital city of Sweden, and I went into a bookshop there and asked for the Gospels. They showed me a complete King James Bible. That surprised me: the Jewish Old Testament together in one book with the Christian New Testament.

When I was alone in my room, I began to read. When I came to John 8:31 and 32, 'To the Jews who had believed in him, Jesus said, "If you hold to my teaching, you are really my disciples. Then you will know the truth, and the truth will set you free."'

Suddenly the room was filled with the presence of God. The Holy Spirit filled me and I had a revelation. First, I saw that my whole life had been moving further and further away from God. My lifestyle was in complete defiance of God. In other words, I saw my own sinfulness. I saw how far I had strayed away from God. I saw that all the problems that exist in the world, from the smallest personal problem to the greatest political crisis, are rooted in the separation between God and humanity. All problems stem from this separation.

I further saw that Jesus not only suffered physical pain on the cross, but experienced the whole of the suffering of mankind in the past, present and future.

Then I saw that Christ, the Messiah, is my life. I didn't fully understand this revelation. I was overwhelmed by it and couldn't comprehend it. Then I decided to look at it from within my Jewish background.

The way in which I wanted to do this was to go to Israel and to talk with the rabbis. I said to my wife, who was then expecting our first child, 'I'm going to Israel. I don't know when I'll be back, or if I'll be back; but I have to go.' The Christmas season was just beginning when I left.

On arrival in Israel I enrolled myself in a *Yeshiva*, an Orthodox religious Jewish school in Jerusalem. Immediately I began to ask the rabbis questions about Jesus. Two of them wanted me to tear the New Testament out of my Bible. One of them wanted to speak to me in secret, but nothing came of it because I left the *Yeshiva*. I was trying to get answers to urgent questions, but the *Yeshiva* didn't have any answers for me.

I stayed in Israel for two months and worked in different kibbutzim.

It never occurred to me to go to a church. Christianity didn't interest me at all. But I had got as far as knowing that Yeshua is the Messiah. I couldn't comprehend what that meant and still hadn't accepted him. No one had explained the gospel to me.

I went back to Sweden and we both felt that something was about to happen. My wife wrote on a piece of paper in Swedish, 'We are waiting for the ignition spark,' and she pinned it to the wall in the kitchen. We had a very confused view of spiritual life and mixed belief in God with Eastern mysticism.

For one reason or another we believed that the people in

England lived a more spiritual life than those in Sweden. We said, 'If God gives us a certain amount of money, we will see that as a sign that we are to go to England.' Then we thought of an amount that would be impossible for us to get together in six months.

In those days I gave music lessons at a school in Stockholm. My subject was contemporary music. Within six months we had double the amount that we had thought of.

We were vegetarians and our plan was to start a bio-dynamic farm in England. So we got rid of everything we possessed, selling as much as possible and giving the rest away, and then left for England.

But everything went wrong. Wherever we went every door was closed. People we expected to meet didn't turn up and . . . it rained constantly. We were still wearing our Swedish winter clothes, although it was summer in England. But that summer in England was colder than winter in Sweden. It was a damp sort of cold, penetrating everything. It rained for six long weeks and our money was fast running out.

We thought, 'Perhaps we can go to Canada.' I was hesitant about going back to the United States because I thought that the FBI would be looking for me in relation to my military service, although when I left America I still hadn't been called up. My parents believed that the FBI wanted to bring me back to the US because I had to do military service. Later it became evident that they only wanted to know where I was living. For years I thought that the FBI were on my heels.

Instead of Canada, we ended up in Denmark. We had thought when we left, 'We won't be back in Scandinavia for ten years,' but after six weeks there we were again. Again we tried to find a farm where we could grow vegetables organically. But that didn't work out.

So we travelled on further, to Sweden, and stayed with

my parents-in-law. After a while my father-in-law began to ask awkward questions, like, 'How do you think you will be able to support your family?' I couldn't take that and said, 'We're leaving.' So on the third day we reloaded the little car that I had bought in England, and drove to the city of Lund where I had first met my wife.

We were walking through the streets, looking for a place to spend the night, when I met an old friend. He wanted to take us to a house where they played heavy music and used drugs, but we weren't interested in that any more.

We walked further and came to a house with a small sign in the window, on which was written in Swedish, 'Jesus is the way, the truth and the life.' That touched my heart and I thought, 'If they really believe in Jesus there, they'll offer us a place to stay.'

So I knocked on the door, but no one opened it.

I went round the back and knocked on the back door. A young woman opened it and I told her that we were looking for somewhere to sleep. She asked, 'Do you believe in Jesus?'

I said, 'Yes.' But we believed in a lot of things.

'Oh, come in then,' she said.

So we had a bed and we thought, 'Tomorrow we'll move on further north, where friends we know own a biodynamic farm.'

The following day we phoned our friends who told us that their house was full and they couldn't have us. So we stayed another night in that house.

The next day a group of young people who had been to a conference came in. They were brimming over with the joy of the Lord. We asked them all sorts of questions and for the very first time got answers that meant something to us. We understood that they had found the truth which we were looking for.

They explained the gospel to us: that we had to turn from our sins and ask Jesus to come into our hearts. We asked that then in a simple prayer. At once we experienced the Holy Spirit cleansing our hearts. It was as if our insides took a good shower.

A few days later we were baptised. They prayed with us and we were baptised in the Holy Spirit. We were filled with joy. It was like being on a honeymoon with the Lord.

There were in total fifteen people living in that house; among them were alcoholics and drug addicts who had come to know the Lord. We went to conferences with these young people and got good biblical teaching. We saw miracles happen. We enjoyed the meetings in which God was praised. That's how our new life began. Instead of staying one day, my wife and I and our baby lived in that small room for eight months.

One day my wife had a vision. She saw that our life was going to change. The Lord would take us back to America or to Israel. She couldn't make out when or what period of time was involved. It seemed an impossible task—Israel as much as America. But the changes began within a few days and three weeks later we were already in the United States, where we stayed for one and a half years.

I prayed from time to time that the Lord would show me if he had any special purpose for me as a Jew. For others it was something special that I, as a Jew, believed in Jesus, but to me it didn't have any special significance. I had already been to Israel once and I hoped never in my life to have to go there again.

In 1983 the Lord started to wake me up night after night, showing me verses in the Bible that speak about the return of the Jews to their land. I thought about Psalms 120 to 134, which are called 'songs of ascents'. I had never noticed that there was a footnote in the Bible I was using which tells how these psalms were sung by pilgrims on the way to Jerusalem. Something began to stir in me.

Suddenly I had a longing to start learning Hebrew. When I opened my Bible, I invariably saw texts about the return of the Jews to Israel. I kept coming across verses about God's special love for Jerusalem. This love grew and grew.

In 1984 the Lord quickened Philippians 2:13 to me, which says that God is working in you, making you willing and able to do his good will. I understood that God doesn't always give a command when he asks us to do something, but that he works in our hearts so that we will be pleased to do it.

I got to the point that I didn't want to live anywhere else but in Israel. We came here in July 1985.

We came just with faith, nothing else. I had no prospect of a job or support from overseas and we then had six children. In Sweden I felt that the Lord was asking me to give all my possessions away. I mustn't sell them, but give them away. So we came here with only a few toys for the children. We were able to live in the absorption centre and went to the *ulpan* to learn the language.

In a miraculous way God provided so that we could stay in the absorption centre for two years. I could write a book about all the miracles that the Lord did for us.

I found a job in a factory where they made laser lenses. I had to polish the lenses.

Then the Lord laid it on my heart to go and spread the gospel, but I didn't know how. At a conference about evangelism in a holiday centre in the north of Israel I shared a room with Kelvin Crombi, who worked as a historian at Christ Church. I heard from him that they needed someone as receptionist in the church; only you weren't paid for it. You would greet people who came to the church and be available to talk with them.

Because I had no work then I took it on. So that's how I came to Christ Church and later became the manager of the bookshop, which I still am today.

People told me, when I came here, that it is possible to

evangelise in any other city in Israel, but not in Jerusalem. But I see it differently.

At first I just went out on to the streets, spoke to people and distributed Hebrew tracts which explained the gospel alongside texts from the Old Testament.

Many people think that it is illegal to spread the gospel here, but that isn't true. It is forbidden to bribe an adolescent to change religion.

I was once fined because I handed out tracts on the street. But the courts threw out the charge because there is no law which forbids the distributing of tracts or the preaching of the gospel.

Of course, sometimes you are threatened, and I have ended up in some difficult situations, but most of the experiences on the street have been positive.

Others think that you have to be a Jew yourself to be able to speak to Jews; that also is not true. It says in Romans 11 that God will use the Gentiles to make the Jews jealous. Many Jews have come to faith through the witness of a Gentile.

There have also been negative reactions, but more than 90 per cent have been positive. By the way, I see a much greater receptiveness developing.

We have had many good conversations. Some Orthodox as well as unbelieving Jews ask straight out if Jesus really is the Jewish Messiah and want to know more about it.

We know that there are Chassidic Jews who believe in Jesus in secret. I have spoken with ultra-Orthodox Jews on the street who can't discount the possibility that Jesus really is the Messiah. An especially strong working of the Spirit is needed to bring them to the point where they can confess that Yeshua is the Messiah. But I believe that this is going to happen.

It is a mystery to me too, what it means to be a Jew. Maybe I'll only really know when I meet the Lord.

When the disciples in Luke 10 came back after they had

performed great miracles in the name of the Lord, Jesus told them not to rejoice over this, 'but rejoice that your names are written in heaven' (v 20). That means to me: your identity is recorded in heaven. Your real name, your real identity stands written in heaven. Many Jewish people take a new name when they enter the country. I didn't feel the need to do that because a new name is waiting for me in heaven.

There are many Jewish believers who express their identity as a Jew by keeping the old traditions and rituals. I don't feel led to do that, maybe because my wife is Swedish and not Jewish. Our marriage is a witness to the fact that God has broken down the dividing wall between Jews and Gentiles.

I feel that my Jewishness is expressed in the fact that the Lord has called me to live in Israel. This is my home, I want to live here. I am one of the many Jews from whose heart the veil has been removed and who can see Jesus as the Messiah; who haven't gone over to another religion, but in fact have found their real Jewish roots in him.

We have the promises. It is only a question of time and 'all Israel shall be saved'. That has to happen before the Messiah comes. The day will come when all Jews will know him.

There is a theological viewpoint which says, 'You don't need to witness to the Jews because they will all be saved anyway.' I don't believe that, because Paul in Romans 1:16 says, 'I am not ashamed of the gospel, because it is the power of God for the salvation of everyone who believes: first for the Jew, then for the Gentile.' I know that I was not saved simply because I had that wonderful vision. I also had to hear the gospel from another person. People who have special experiences still need to hear the gospel and make a conscious decision in response to it. Paul met Jesus on the way to Damascus, but it was also necessary for

Ananias to come and explain the gospel to him. God therefore uses human instruments.

In 2 Corinthians 5:18 it says that we are God's representatives to bring reconciliation. As soon as we are born again, we have to begin to spread the gospel and so work towards the reconciliation between God and man.

9
Israel, the Wounded One

Israel Harel is a real evangelist who doesn't let himself be held back by anything.

He himself is the fruit of straight-from-the-shoulder evangelism. When he was a young drug addict, living with a group of hippies in the alcoves of the old city walls of Jerusalem, an American lady broke all the rules and witnessed in plain terms to him about Jesus. Israel owes his life to that.

When Israel sat beside me, telling his story into my little cassette recorder, I thought, 'When do we learn to accept the omnipotence of God, and his ability to lead everyone in a different way?' Some Jews come to the knowledge that Jesus is the Messiah by revelation. God uses dreams, visions and all kinds of revelations. But he also uses people. Sometimes even the most unlikely. We narrow the wisdom and creativity of our God by putting up theological barriers. He is not impressed and just goes on reaching out to people in need through everyone who is obedient and willing to go.

I was born in the kibbutz Chulda between Rehovot and Jerusalem. When I was still very young, we moved to the kibbutz Ayelet Hashachar. Both my parents were also born in Israel.

The greater part of my youth was spent in the *moshav* Sde Moshe in the Lachish area. I lived there until I was fifteen.

It was a normal, worldly *moshav*. But there was respect for the Bible at the school. When you live in this country, you know that the Bible speaks about real things, even if you don't believe in God.

Even so, God's name was almost never mentioned in our house. We were critical of Orthodox Judaism. Now I can see for myself that they had wandered away from the simplicity of the Bible. I can compare them with the Roman Catholics, who worship their saints. They pray at the graves of great rabbis and honour them as saints. Their interpretation of the law is given the same authority as God's word.

We had our own piece of land in the *moshav* and our own house, but other things were done co-operatively, such as the purchasing and the running of the nursery school. My parents didn't get on very well together and as a child I suffered because of that. My father had himself never experienced a warm parental home, so he didn't know how to be a good father.

My mother was seventeen when she had me! So she didn't really know how to be a good mother either. She was still a child herself. Her mother had had the same problem and so had her grandmother.

Farming didn't really appeal to my parents, so my mother broke loose and took up teaching. She was an excellent teacher. She taught children who had had a difficult start in life, but her talent didn't extend to her own home. As my father didn't have much interest in farming, he never had much money either. This resulted in my becoming rebellious from a very early age. I reacted to the problems at home with increasing insubordination.

Growing up in a closed community everyone knew everything about you, so you gained a reputation that wasn't easy to get rid of. You had to do things together with your contemporaries. After school we worked together in the fields, drove the tractor and joined in the evening activities of the youth movement. The group reinforced the rejection that I received at home. I was weak inside and my friends took advantage of it.

Our *moshav* wasn't very far from the old city of Lachish, which is mentioned in the Bible. It is beautiful there. It is the point where the coastal plain meets the rolling Judean hills. There are many vineyards and orchards. We cultivated potatoes, tomatoes and cucumbers. In fact, it was a wonderful place to grow up in.

I did well and got good grades at junior school, but at secondary school I had to repeat my studies and I'd never learned how to do that. I had to resit the third year and after that I left school and transferred to an agricultural school in Ashdod.

I was a boarder there, which brought me into contact with a different culture. There were American youngsters at the school and they had hash and played rock music. It was in the period just after Woodstock—the time of peace demonstrations and flower power.

I was kicking against society and the hypocrisy of the older generation, which said one thing but did another. When questioned, the reply was, 'That is what society demands.' I asked, 'Who is society?' In my opinion, society was sick.

My father told me, 'You'll never amount to anything.' So I decided to prove him right. Everything I did would be different to the accepted norm. I made that my life's pattern: always do everything differently.

Four days before the end of the school year I left Achziv

in the north and went to Eilat in the south, which in those days was the place where all the hippies could be found.

There was a *wadi* there, where we lived in huts and used drugs. We told each other that drugs were the answer to the problems of the world, because when young people are stoned, they are everybody's friend and are in a state of euphoria. That means peace and that's how the new world will come about. So we lay on the beach all day and got stoned in the evening and slept off our high ready to begin again the next day.

Sometimes I caught the bus and went to visit my parents, but mostly it ended up with a big row and then I left again. My father would ask, 'What do you do all day?' I told him that we would lie on the beach thinking things over. I was still only fifteen years old.

In winter I lived on the beach in Eilat and in summer, in the park in Tel Aviv. We picked up American girls on the Dizingof Square every other day and went to bed with them. There were always groups of American girls to choose from.

When I was eighteen I moved to Jerusalem. We lived with a group of hippies in and around the walls of the old city. There are alcoves there, which were designed for the archers, and we slept in them. I heard mention of the name Jesus for the first time there, through a sect who called themselves Children of God. They gathered around my girlfriend and me and began singing: 'You've got to be like children to go to heaven.' It seemed like brainwashing. I didn't want to have anything to do with it.

Rina Jackwith, an American lady, also came to us there. She broke all the rules; she had never heard of being cautious, which was my good fortune, otherwise I wouldn't be here any more.

I can't understand how people can say they have a love for Israel and yet won't share the treasure in their heart—

Jesus. I find it a form of anti-Semitism if you don't pass on Jesus to the Jews. This evangelistic, white-haired lady always carried a King James Bible around with her. She was old fashioned and fanatical. She belonged to a church that believed in dispensationalism. For her, the Bible consisted of different parts: that part is the past, that for the future, Paul's letters are for now, and so on. We, as Jews, came out reasonably well. I didn't understand any of it.

This lady invited us to her home as she wanted to give us something to eat. There were eight of us hippies and that really appealed to us. There was only one condition: we were not allowed to smoke in her house and we had to listen to a Bible study. But if you get free food, you can put up with that. Besides, it was winter. Perhaps this way we could also get a place to sleep.

Lovingly she opened her house to us and cooked for us. She kept saying that we had to be born again. She showed us a beaker and poured water into it from a can. The Spirit of God had to come into your heart like that. I don't remember exactly how it went. But we thought that she told it well.

She also made us read prophecies from the *Tenach*: Isaiah 53, Jeremiah 31 and Ezekiel 36, and she claimed that only Jesus could fulfil these prophecies.

We were allowed to live in her house for two weeks. She put the question to us: 'Okay, do you believe or not?' We thought, 'If we say no, she'll throw us out and we won't have anything to eat and it's cold outside,' so we said, 'Yes we believe.'

Young people who use drugs will do anything for a meal. But there was more to it for me. I thought about what she had said about the Messiah and Jesus. Especially about Isaiah 53:9 where it says that he 'had done no violence, nor was any deceit in his mouth'. That couldn't refer to Israel, for that is full of sin. Up to the time of Rabbi Rashi (1040–1105), a famous Bible interpreter from Troyes in France, the generally accepted interpretation was that this text referred to the Messiah. But now it is held to refer to Israel.

I realised that I would have to give everything to Jesus if I accepted him. For me that didn't mean giving up my time, because I had all the time in the world. Nor money, because I didn't have any. He wanted more than that: my ambitions, my dreams, my inner self, my will. And I would have to be obedient, which I found the most difficult. I didn't want anyone telling me what I should do, not even God.

So I walked away from God and went back to Eilat. We didn't have heroine in those days, so I began injecting opium and became addicted to LSD. The strange thing was that these drugs no longer gave me the same kick as before. Something inside me had discovered a criterion against which all my experiences were measured. I had seen something of the truth and knew that I was walking away from it.

To get high, I began using more and more. At first I was injecting once a month, then once a week, three times a week, and then daily. My brains were exploding and I was burned out. So I swallowed more pills to pep myself up. It was hopeless.

I had a longing to go to Europe. I had earned some money by managing my father's kiosk and flew to Holland.

When I arrived in Amsterdam, I thought, 'This is heaven, because anything goes here.' I began dealing in drugs myself in the Vondelpark. But the upshot of that was that I ended up desolate and lonely in the park. The police picked me up, so I was arrested and thrown out of the country.

Back in Israel, I began dealing in drugs again and was arrested within the shortest possible time. I had already been picked up once before and released on probation. So now that I had been picked up for the second time, I could get at least a six-year prison sentence.

In the meantime, my friend with whom I had been on the beach in Eilat, the Dutchman John Pex, had come to faith. According to the law, I would have to go to prison because I'd been picked up for drugs for the second time. But when we were sitting in the courtroom, the judge forgot to call me. John, who was waiting outside, was praying.

At the end of the session I went to the judge and said, 'Excuse me, but you forgot to call me.'

He said, 'Come with me to my office.'

I went inside, together with the prosecutor, a woman who was representing the police. The judge sat behind an impressive desk with all the law books behind him.

I began praying silently, 'Oh Lord, I really don't want to go to prison. It's terrible, I know that from experience.'

The judge reflected for a moment and said, 'I'll give you another three years' probation and a fine of 450 shekels.'

I couldn't believe my ears and went straight outside to John; we both danced around and praised God. We were really happy, but that didn't last for long.

I fell back into my old lifestyle again. Not twice, but three or four times. I lived in the park in Tel Aviv. At night I stole alcohol from the supermarket and in the morning I sold it. With the money, I bought food. I slept on a bench and sometimes begged for money. I sank lower and lower.

My family disowned me. I was the black sheep of the family. I hadn't done military service, I used drugs, was a hippy and gave the family a bad name.

I couldn't maintain lasting relationships. The bitterness always came back to the surface.

My friends in the park also turned away from me. After my father, my mother and all of society had turned their backs on me, they were followed by the friends with whom I'd been involved day-in day-out.

I said to myself, 'If no one will accept me as I am, then I'll commit suicide.' I had a little money so I went to all the chemists in Tel Aviv and bought every sleeping tablet that was available without a prescription. I resolved, 'I'll swallow all these pills and if I don't wake up any more, well—goodbye world. If I do wake up, then I'll call the probation officer, whom the court said I had to see every now and then and ask to be admitted to a psychiatric institution.'

I slept the whole night and woke up as usual the following day; nothing had happened. Because you could get these pills without a prescription, they weren't very strong; besides, my body was accustomed to drugs. So I called my social worker and was admitted.

I spent seven months in the institution at Askelon, and after that, two years in Etanim near Jerusalem. I was a schizophrenic paranoid patient, who constantly tried to commit suicide. I smashed glass windows and attacked people. I also had a Bible next to me and told everyone that I believed in Jesus. But I still did not belong to him. Every time I tried to read the Bible, something happened. It really was a demonic situation there.

The doctors and nurses surrounded me with every care and I liked it, because if you're crazy, you can't be held responsible for anything. The doctor told my mother that I would have to spend the rest of my life in such institutions —I was incurable.

But still God protected me. One day I swallowed a handful of pills and they were very strong pills. As a result I lay unconscious and tied to my bed for two weeks. I had to be watched day and night.

There was a doctor there who abused his position in order to dominate people. He told lies about me which made me furious. One day I saw a knife lying on the floor in the kitchen. I ran in and reached out my hand to grab the knife, but found myself holding a fork instead. I threw it at the doctor and the fork hit him on his forehead. If I had thrown the knife, it would have turned out much worse. The doctor had a wound which needed four stitches. It was the last straw.

The police were called and a complaint was filed against me. I had to leave the institution immediately. That was the best thing that could have happened to me. Now I was out and free of the melancholy atmosphere. I had to make decisions for myself. I was twenty-three and had the key to the street, but where could I go? Not to my family. My father hadn't wanted to speak to me for two years and declared me dead. My friends didn't want to have anything to do with me either.

The institution was situated between wooded hills; it was beautiful there. I walked into the woods with the intention of ending my life. I had taken a belt and with that I was going to hang myself. As I was on the way to a deserted spot, I was checked by an invisible figure. It was a tangible, physical, but invisible figure. I couldn't go any further.

I was in such a deep darkness that I decided to stop eating and kill myself that way. I went and sat under a tree and thought, 'I'm going to sit here until I die.'

I had my Bible with me, which I never read. Now I had plenty of time. I started reading. I don't know what I read any more, but suddenly a stream of light came out of the Bible and right into me. I sat reading like that for eight days, until peace had permeated my heart. I had a certainty that everything would turn out all right. This was the first time in the two and a half years that I had been in the institution that I had such a certainty. Suddenly there was this peace, as though the storm had passed by. Rest, deep inner rest. How glorious that was. But what should I do next?

All at once I knew: I had to find John, otherwise I would lose this newly found peace. I found John and we travelled to Eilat together. John was already bringing many people to the Lord. He wanted to start a hostel where people could hear the gospel.

I helped John and also witnessed myself. But as I testified that Jesus can set us free, I was taking a puff of my cigarette every couple of sentences, because I smoked three packets a day. On the inside I was still full of bitterness and I still felt rejected.

In my Bible I read all sorts of things about the end times. I thought, 'The past never comes back, we can't change the present, so only the future is important. Let's study the prophecies.' I received a large sum of money by being paid a year's arrears of benefit. 'That's that,' I said to myself. 'Now it's time to leave. I'm going to go away from here, away from people. I'll go to the island of Patmos and live on fish, and perhaps the atmosphere will still be the same as in the time of John, who received the Book of Revelation there. Perhaps Jesus will show me when he's coming back.'

I found a boat in Haifa that was leaving for Cyprus; from there I could take a boat to Patmos. I reserved a bunk in a four-berth cabin. It was winter and not very pleasant on deck. So I went to my cabin and introduced myself to the three other men who would be sleeping there. One of them asked, 'What do you do?'

I answered, 'I travel.'

'Why?'

I said, 'To look for something.'

'What have you found so far?'

And to their utter amazement I answered, 'God.'

'Moses?'

'No,' I said, 'Jesus.'

Suddenly they were very enthusiastic and said that they also believed in Jesus, and in speaking in tongues, and in healing. In my short career as a Christian, I had heard all sorts of arguments against speaking in tongues and faith healing, so I said, 'That's not biblical.' The conversation degenerated into a verbal dispute. We spoke louder and louder and beat each other with Bible verses. Looking back, we weren't exactly an example of brotherly love.

During this heated discussion, two things pierced my heart like an arrow. One said, 'Why do you put God in your own little box and put him on a shelf to look at? Why don't you say to God, "Show me who you are?"'

A little later I said, 'Let me hear that crazy babbling.' And one of them spoke a few sentences in tongues out loud. I heard that it was a real language, not babble. It touched me deeply, but I wasn't about to show that.

These young men told me that they had to take a couple of minibuses to a place in Cyprus—Skouriotissa or something like that. It was some school or other, but I didn't understand all the details.

At six o'clock in the morning, we sailed into the port of Limassol. The four of us stood on deck and watched them mooring the ship and I wanted to ask them if I could go with them. I knew that God was giving me a last chance. I had been running away from him for six years now, and yet I couldn't escape him. I had long hair, wore earrings, had boots on and wore a long coat. A real hippy.

I thought, 'If I don't go with them and if nothing radical happens to me, I'll spend the rest of my life wandering through the streets of Limassol like someone possessed.' It was like Nebuchadnezzar's insanity in the Book of Daniel. I was afraid that I would go the same way. I thought, 'If they refuse me, it won't be my fault that I turn my back on God. Then I'll crawl back into my shell again and feel rejected as usual.' So I stepped up to them and asked if I could go with them. To my surprise they said, 'Yes, of course.'

The journey across Cyprus took two hours. You drive along the coast then you get more and more into mountainous country. We were constantly getting lost and having to ask directions from people at small farms.

At one particular point I saw an enormous mountain of stones and rubble—the old copper mine. They told me that this copper mine already existed in the year 500 BC and that it had been worked continually since then. After the Turkish invasion in 1974, the mine and the buildings were managed by the Greek Orthodox Church. Youth With A Mission—a youth missionary organisation—rented the buildings from the church.

When we drove on to the property, children playing there came towards us. One of the men spoke with the leader and asked if I might stay. Once again I heard, 'You're welcome.'

I knew with my mind quite a few things about God and the Bible, but I still had little personal experience of him.

That evening they had a meeting in a small hall. There was a speaker who was of Catholic origin, very conservative. He said, 'I feel that there is someone here who needs prayer.' I thought, 'Here we go.' But I also thought, 'I've come this far, I can't walk away any more.' So I let them lay their hands on me and they began to pray.

And then I saw the Lord. I realised that he had been following me for years, to tell me that he loved me and I had spat in his face time and again, saying, 'Just let me go my own way.'

The Lord said, 'I love you. I'm standing here behind you with open arms.' I broke down in tears and called out, 'Lord, everything in my life is going downhill. My family don't want to know me any more, my friends have deserted me. I'm full of bitterness, have suicidal tendencies. There isn't anyone anywhere who can help me now, only you, oh Lord.'

I had admitted defeat. It was as if a black blanket was pulled off me. I could really see and feel this blanket just fall off my shoulders and disappear. In the days that followed, I felt ten kilos lighter. I had lost my burden of guilt, sin and bitterness.

I very much wanted to stay at the base for a while and that was permitted. It was a strange situation. You could find young people from all the surrounding countries here— Egypt, Jordan, even Syria—and there was I in their midst, a Jew. Everyone was enthusiastic about Jesus. The people working in the vegetable garden sang songs while working. If you worked on the farm, then you praised the Lord there. It was the time of the first love and people had great visions about spreading the gospel to every country in the Middle East.

I once bumped into a woman and said, 'Forgive me.' 'Of course I forgive you. This and everything,' she said. I didn't understand that. Then she explained to me that the Holy Spirit can live in you and that you can forgive in the power of the Spirit. I thought, 'That's what I need.' But I didn't want them to lay hands on me and pray again. I wanted to experience it alone with God.

In my room I was reading my Bible and suddenly it was as if I'd lost contact with the ground while a whole waterfall was being poured out over my head. This waterfall of pure light washed over me. I was bathed in God's love. It seemed as if this love went right through me, flowing through my body to come out again through my pores. It washed me clean. I felt as if God was embracing me like a Father. I had finally come home.

Later the Lord showed me that he was being very careful in showing me his love because I was like a rusty electrical wire; I couldn't carry too much current all at once.

I became addicted to him. Everything I did was accompanied by praise. I sang the whole day and felt close to the presence of God. There was a meeting every evening and I went there every time and sang along with the songs, as loudly as possible. I had received the spirit of joy and when

I didn't know the words any more, I received words in an unintelligible language.

On the boat to Cyprus I had bought a carton of cigarettes. But I realised that I had to stop smoking. So I went to a brook and threw all the precious cigarettes into it.

Now I still had to learn how to live. Is there a school in existence where you can learn how to start a new life? God placed me in his school.

The first lesson I learned was to forgive. I forgave my parents.

I went to the hairdresser and had my long hair cut off.

I went along in the little van on a trip to Nicosia to buy food and bought different clothes.

I had my photo taken and sent a copy to John in Eilat. He wrote that they couldn't believe it was me.

I wrote a letter to the psychologists at my psychiatric institution, and their reaction was, 'What's happened?'

After one year, during which I completed various training courses, I went back to Tel Aviv. A small congregation worshipped at Immanuel House, and there I met other believers. I went to work there as a volunteer in the office of their hostel.

I also met my Swiss wife, Brigitte, there and we got married.

There were more and more Messianic believers in Tel Aviv. The Dugit bookshop in Frishman Street was a meeting place and a centre for evangelism.

More and more activities were developing in the centre of the country. But we wanted to become pioneers. We wanted to work in new areas, where everything still had to get off the ground. So we established ourselves in Tivon.

I see it as a fishing net. The threads are the relationships which connect the congregations all over the country to each other. If the spiritual bond isn't there, the fishing net doesn't work.

God wants to make small congregations grow and spread over the whole country, joined to each other like a fishing net. Satan doesn't think much of this. He sticks his knife in the net and tries to rip it so that we can't fish. We don't need a unified organisation, but a unity of heart, a unified tuning-in to the Spirit.

10

Avi, the Compassionate

Beersheba bakes in the hot desert sun. The *sharav* doesn't let up and yellow dust pushes its way into everything. Luckily the bus from Tel Aviv has good air conditioning. On arrival at the bus station in Beersheba I phone Avi Magid. 'I'll be right with you,' he says.

I buy the latest edition of the *Jerusalem Post* with the most recent news about the Gulf crisis and saunter across the road to the weekly Bedouin market with a falafel in my hand—always a colourful spectacle. Men with blue and white or red and white *kaseyahs* on their heads and women in long robes. They have yellow-brown skin, or sometimes are a burned dark brown, and make large gestures when buying or selling. Camels and donkeys walk between the stalls on which are sold rugs, pots and pans and awful souvenirs for the tourists. It is a colourful and noisy world.

A taxi stops. A man with a grey beard and a pair of dark-rimmed glasses gets out—it must be Avi Magid (sixty-two). He greets me in Dutch. You don't expect that here in the Negev, close to the Bedouins.

I get into the taxi and we drive past the modern post

TWELVE JEWS DISCOVER MESSIAH

office and the university to a suburb. The desert is always
present. Every now and then you see the barren infinity
between the buildings.

As we enter the small three-roomed flat, we're almost
knocked over by three dogs which have just been let out.
Unbelievable! Such a small flat for a family of five and three
dogs!

But I haven't been told the half of it yet. Avi and his wife
Esther take drug addicts into their family. On top of all this
they take care of a severely handicapped baby, who needs
liquid nourishment every twenty minutes.

As a result of their constant care for this small child who
is deaf, blind and paralysed, they can never go away for the
day, and definitely cannot go on a holiday.

I get one surprise after another. We go inside and Avi
disappears into the tiny kitchen. He calls through the open
door, 'I've had a packet of Douwe Egberts coffee here for
months, a present from someone, for a special occasion.
Shall I make some real Dutch coffee? Would you like some?'

What a question! I sit on the sofa and wait patiently,
taking a look around. There is a large aquarium, and
one of Avi's paintings—a town with picturesque, ochre-
coloured houses—hangs on the wall. Avi comes in with the
coffee and explains that he is really a painter, 'But I don't
have the time any more to make anything beautiful, because
we're so busy looking after drug addicts.'

I start my cassette recorder, and Avi begins. In the
background you can hear the regular breathing of the three
sleeping dogs, the rattly breathing of the paralysed baby,
and the voice of one of the addicts who's come to ask
something.

I was born in Rotterdam. My mother was a Jewess. My
father was a doctor who specialised in tropical diseases. He
wasn't a Jew. I was the only child. Apart from my mother
and me, no one else from our family survived the war.

In 1942 the oppression by the occupiers became much more severe and we had to wear a yellow star. One day, when I was eleven years old, my mother was stopped in the street because she wasn't wearing her yellow star, and didn't have her identity papers with her either. She was arrested and brought home. While the German soldiers were standing in the room, they noticed a photo of me on the mantelpiece and asked, 'Who is that?'

My mother said, 'That is my son, but he isn't here now.' The soldiers wanted to know where I was, but my mother refused to tell them. Then they beat her until she cried out that I was at school.

They went to my school and informed the headmaster, 'We've come to take Avi Magid.' The headmaster refused, and sent the soldiers away. But the Germans came back and told him that my mother had said that I was to go home, which was a lie.

When the headmaster let me go, I was arrested and taken away. My mother and I were taken to the police head-quarters. By the time evening came they had obviously rounded up enough prisoners because we were then moved to a large shed on the Stieltjesplein. In this shed, the Germans assembled the people to be taken by train to the concentration camps. The conditions in these sheds were terrible. People cried, some were beaten, and you knew that what followed would be much worse. The SS committed the most awful crimes right in front of my eyes. I was eleven years old, and I saw them beat people to death. For the very first time I was confronted with death.

In July 1942 we were transported by train to Westerbork camp in Drente, one of the rural provinces in the north of Holland. In 1942 the Germans occupied this crowded camp, and gave it the awful name of Judendurchgangslager. Here they imprisoned a total of 106,537 Jews and some hundreds of gypsies.

Every Tuesday a transport train (without windows)

departed for the extermination camps in Germany and Poland. This was called the Himmelfahrtstrasse, the street to heaven. For 102,000 Jews this was indeed the last train. First you saw the large ditch and barbed wire fences, then the many wooden barracks painted in a rusty brown. The area at the southeast side was used for the daily roll call.

It was almost night when my mother and I arrived, so I did not see much of the place. German soldiers pushed our miserable group inside the gate. I saw the watchtowers beside the fence.

Suddenly everyone was in a hurry. I don't know why. Perhaps those at the rear were just fearful that they would be beaten, and pushed the rest inside.

What I feared most happened then: I was separated from my mother. I had never been away from my mother until that moment. Mother was for me the only link with home and life. I thought, 'This is the most miserable day of my life.' I was pushed towards a barrack with wooden bunks, three-high. Another boy of my age, Japie van Kleef, also from Rotterdam, got the bunk above mine. But he was a bed-wetter. And that is not pleasant when you have the lower bunk!

Next morning the soldiers ordered us out of bed for the roll call. I learned that you had to stand up straight, however long it might take, and that if you looked around you were struck. It was so confusing and discouraging. Grown-ups spoke out loud of their fears about death. Every day could be the day that you were put 'on transport' and we knew already that that meant death. They spoke aloud of their fears and did not realise what a devastating impression that made on the children, who think that grown-ups have all the right answers.

The Germans discovered that my mother was a nurse, so she was put to work in another barrack.

During the six months of our stay, from July until the end of December 1942, it grew colder and colder and we wore the only clothes we had, those that we wore on the day we were transported. There was no heating in the barracks, and life became grimmer and grimmer. Some prisoners got special rights; somehow they earned some money and could buy things in the 'camp shop'. But we had no money and no privileges. They didn't beat me there, but I sat in constant fear because I knew we were to be sent on to Poland or Germany.

Then the amazing thing happened—we got a chance to escape. It happened like this. I was sitting in the barracks when my mother entered and took me aside. She told me that the gate was open, and that we could escape. Probably the military policeman had gone outside for a moment, leaving the gate open. Whether he did that deliberately or by mistake we've never known. We walked to the big steel gate, topped with barbed wire, and saw it ajar. 'Let's go,' my mother said, but I hesitated. I was afraid. But my mother was able to convince me, so we slipped out of the camp.

The road leading to the camp was a rough, narrow lane, used by farmers to reach their fields. We were free, but the fear of being discovered took away any joy. If a car with Germans should come up the road, we would have been caught and then been worse off. We walked fifteen minutes and froze: there was a car coming.

Two Dutch policemen sat in the car and my only thought was, 'They're going to take us back to the camp.' But one policeman whispered something to the other and then said, 'Quick, come with us,' and bundled us into the car.

We didn't know where they would take us. We hadn't gone very far when two men in civilian clothing stopped us.

'This doesn't look good,' one policeman said. The two men were Dutch Nazis.

They asked, 'Who are the woman and the boy there? Aren't they Jews?'

The policeman confirmed this. Then he said as an

afterthought, 'Er . . . we have to take them to Assen for questioning.'

The Dutch Nazis swallowed this and let us pass. The policemen did, in fact, take us to Assen, but not to the occupiers. They drove to the house of a man from the resistance and asked him if he would help us further.

When we got out of the car, my mother again asked the names of the policemen who had saved our lives. She said, 'When the war is over, we will repay you.' But they refused to give their names, which was of course understandable for their own safety. After the liberation we tried to trace the two policemen, but we never succeeded in finding them.

The man from the resistance took us to the train the next day and said that someone would be waiting for us at the station in Rotterdam. Another person from the resistance would take us to our hiding place.

We weren't stopped during the train journey, and thus arrived in Rotterdam. The only thing was, we didn't know what the man who was going to meet us looked like.

When the train stopped in Rotterdam, someone came straight to us and asked, 'Have you come from Assen?' We said, 'Yes.' It was then we realised that we were in good hands.

A day later we were taken to Den Haag. There we were separated. My mother went to one hiding place and I to another. Shortly after her arrival at the hiding place my mother was again arrested and put on transport. But she survived—the only one of her family. I would see her again after the war.

When I got to my hiding place, the lady of the house said, 'Young man, the first thing that you're going to do is get some sleep, as you look absolutely exhausted.' She took me to a small bedroom with a neatly made bed, and there I was tucked in. She thought that I'd get some rest straight away, but that just wasn't possible. I still heard the screaming, and saw the most awful things happening before my eyes; things I'd seen in the camp and during the transportation. My head was spinning from all the fear and experiences through which I'd been and I couldn't find any rest.

It was roughly four o'clock in the afternoon, and there was a clear sky. The sun shone into the little room. I sat upright in bed with big fearful eyes, listening in case someone had maybe come to take me away again. I was in a state of utter panic, a state of shock.

While I sat there full of fear, the sunny room suddenly became as black as night. I didn't know what was happening to me. I hadn't actually realised that it had become dark until I saw a figure in the right-hand corner of the room— a glowing figure. I couldn't distinguish a face or other details. Only a shining outline. The arms, which were outlined by a shining edge, pointed in my direction.

When I saw the figure, all my panic disappeared immediately. I was perfectly calm. I wasn't frightened any more. It lasted maybe less than a second, I don't know. But afterwards the room was again as before—sunny and light.

I then clambered out of bed and went downstairs to the living room, where my 'hiding place mother' sat at the table. Very surprised she asked, 'What are you doing? I've just tucked you up in bed.'

The only thing I said was, 'Who is Jesus?'

The lady looked at me in astonishment and said, 'Why do you ask?'

Then I told her what I'd seen.

She was a woman who believed and she said, 'You have seen the Lord. Sit down, and I will tell you who Jesus is.' And she told me about Jesus, that he came to earth to save us and that he is the promised Messiah.

During the days that followed she let me read the Bible and a new world opened up for me. I consciously followed the Lord and thanked him daily for that moment, that most difficult moment of my life, when he appeared to me. I hadn't looked for him; that was impossible because I didn't know him. He sought me.

After the war, when I was reunited with my mother, I told her of my experience and said that I wanted to follow Jesus and that I believed in him as our Messiah. She then said to me, 'Son, if you think that it is right, then you have my blessing.'

My mother never really came to belief herself. When I told my mother about Jesus, she would say, 'Jesus must have been a good person.' But she could never open herself up to him and she never actually turned to him. She died in 1983 at the age of eighty-four.

From my hiding place I made contact with a preacher on the Bergsingel in Rotterdam. He gave Bible studies in his home which I attended, and I learned a lot from them.

After the war I completed my education. I went to the academy of design in Rotterdam, and in the evenings I went to the school of music. I played the piano.

Later I transferred to study ergotherapy. I worked for twenty years as an ergotherapist in various hospitals. Ergotherapy is a sort of supplement to physiotherapy. You suggest exercises to help people function more ably when parts of the body are damaged through sickness or by an accident.

I met Esther, we got married and had our first daughter. My wife isn't a Jew. She grew up in a Christian family. Later we emigrated to Israel.

The most important reason for us to establish ourselves finally in Israel was the latent presence and re-emergence of anti-Semitism. The fear that neo-Naziism could again raise its head made us decide to come to Israel ten years ago. We aren't Dutch any more, we have Israeli citizenship.

When we came here, they asked us, 'Where do you want to go?'

I said, 'To Galilee.'

But they might as well not have asked, as there was

nowhere to live there. They told us, 'We've only got houses in the Negev.' So, it was off to the Negev then. That's how we came to live in Beersheba.

We were the first ones to move into a flat in this new district. When we looked out of the window here, we would see camels walking below with Bedouin boys on their backs, and sometimes the door was blocked by herds of sheep tended by Bedouin girls.

But alas, that has all disappeared now through the necessary expansion. We find the atmosphere here to be very good—the openness of the people and the unity they have with each other. Maybe it's because it isn't such a business centre, like Tel Aviv, where everyone's in a hurry, and has to get to his office quickly. They have much less time for social contacts.

If I walk through the town here, everyone greets me, but that is, of course, also because I've lived here for more than ten years. They ask me, 'How's your family? Everything okay?' It's all very good-natured and pleasant.

I worked for the first few years as an ergotherapist before we ended up doing the work that we now do. Our family also increased with two more children.

It was five years ago, in the middle of the night, that Esther shook me awake and said, 'I think that I've had a message from the Lord.' She told me that she'd had a vision that we should open up our house to people in need.

I wasn't too pleased at first that she'd woken me up in the middle of the night, nor was I immediately enthusiastic about the idea of taking people into my house. I said, 'Okay, little one, I'll pray about it in the morning and ask the Lord to confirm it to me and, if possible, to give us a sign.'

That's just what I did, and I came to the conclusion that we indeed had to do it. But I didn't know how. Again I asked the Lord for a sign.

In Beersheba, at seven o'clock that evening, there was a Bible study. I went on ahead of Esther as she still had some things to do for the children. She said, 'You go on ahead, I'll be along in a few minutes.'

Shortly after the meeting had begun, Esther came to get me. She said, 'You have to come back home. A man has knocked on our door asking for help.'

I went home with her straight away, and there sat a man. Without too much thought, he'd picked out a house and rung the door bell because, due to his family circumstances, he'd not known what else to do. He was a drug addict, he had no money, and he asked for shelter. I had received my sign—I could almost say, by telegram.

That was our first drug addict guest, who stayed with us for three months until he was free of his addiction.

We only have three rooms. Our elder daughter gives up her room for every new guest, and our younger daughter is put here in the living room to sleep at night. We push two chairs together to make a bed. By the way, we also sleep in the living room. Our son and elder daughter sleep in the only other small bedroom in bunk beds.

As far as our first drug addict guest is concerned, he's doing really well, and we're in regular contact with him. His family situation has also been restored.

Since then we've kept on getting requests to take in drug addicts, also from official quarters. The social services, the law and the prison system know that we are believers— we've said that from the beginning—and they still accept us completely.

The government in Israel doesn't provide the social programmes that many other countries have. Much has to be done through private initiative. There is simply no money for a programme to fight drugs. Unfortunately we are the only believers who do this—taking in and caring for drug addicts.

Out of the eighteen addicts we've taken into our home over the past years, sixteen have turned out all right. We had to let two go because they weren't motivated. The others now function normally. The average time that someone is with us is three months. During these months, they are in every way a part of the family—that is the intention. Through their drug addiction, they have a total lack of discipline. In every family there have to be rules: getting up on time, enjoying meals three times a day, and so on. By working within a family, they come back into a set pattern.

In the time since we arrived in Israel, our spiritual life has been enriched 100 per cent. We chose to be baptised here, in the Jordan. That was an unforgettable day. We did that here with a special purpose—to begin a whole new life in the Lord's service. I could almost say, to wash away the past and to make ourselves completely open. Since that time, we've gone about the work that the Lord has appointed to us.

Here in Beersheba there is a small congregation of Messianic Jews, a few Arabs who believe, and some believers from the other peoples. We come together every Saturday evening for a service. Besides that, we also have a weekly evening Bible study.

And then we still have Jossy, our foster-son. He will be four this month. He was born healthy, but when he was six months old he choked on a bottle of water. His mother wasn't at home when it happened. When she came home, she found her son clinically dead.

The child was taken to hospital by ambulance, a half hour's journey, and there they managed to bring him back to life; but he had suffered enormous brain damage. He was totally paralysed.

When his parents heard this, they didn't want to take him back. He was blind, deaf and paralysed. He couldn't swallow any more, and therefore had to be artificially fed. His parents left him behind, they couldn't accept him any more. We heard this story from a social worker at the hospital and prayed and asked the Lord what we could do.

The next day we got in touch with the hospital and said, 'Listen, we feel that we should make a warm loving home available for this child.' So Jossy came to live with us.

We are immensely thankful that the Lord has brought him to us to be taken care of. His condition has improved decidedly since he's been with us. He has to be fed with twenty millilitres of liquid nutrition every twenty minutes; that has to be administered through a nasal tube.

But he doesn't grow, due to his brain damage; neither does he put on any weight. But, as you can see, he can now move his arms himself. For some time now he can also hear a little again. He sees the difference between light and dark, but we suspect that he doesn't see more than that.

Look, now he's moving his arms. He couldn't do that at all at first.

We know for sure that God has a plan for this child. A child that was clinically dead and after more than half an hour was brought back to life . . . and is slowly improving. Not through technical means in the hospital but here at home, and above all through the Holy Spirit.

Jossy's life is not meaningless. We experience it as a blessing, that we, through our love for the Messiah, may care for him. Maybe love is the only thing that he can experience. Even though he doesn't hear or see anything, he does clearly experience it.

Esther works half days in an old people's home. That's our most important source of income. An average salary here is 850 shekels per month, but as a rule Esther works mornings, and only occasionally in the afternoon. And prices go up all the time. We don't receive any remuneration for taking in our drug addict guests, as I call them. We share everything with them: what we have and have to do without; they share our lives.

I myself am a painter as you can see. I did these paintings of Jerusalem and I've illustrated two books, a story book about *Pesach* and a book for older children. I've had a couple of exhibitions, but that's not a regular income of course. You could really say that we are poor.

Do I feel myself to be a Messianic Jew? Well, I was Jewish enough to be arrested by the Nazis and to be allowed to live here. When I was a boy, my mother always said that we were Jews, but not religious.

I knew therefore that we were Jews, but I didn't really know what that meant. If I asked her about it, she said, 'Listen to me son, I can't tell you that, it's something that's inside you, that's in your blood.' I've never had a clear explanation. So, if you now ask me if I see myself as a Messianic Jew, I first have to ask myself, 'What is a Jew?' I know that I've been born of a Jewish mother, which means according to the Jewish laws that you're recognised as a Jew. Just like Yeshua, when he came to earth, born of a Jewish mother. I am a follower of him. He has taught me to be compassionate. God will not break a bruised reed, 'and a smouldering wick he will not snuff out' (Is 42:3).

II

Fabio, the Musician

Half an hour's drive from Haifa, in the village of Isfia, the believers gather in the hostel Stella Carmel.

Entering the house, I can hear the singing upstairs. I climb the stairs and see a small hall, filled with adults and children. The floor and walls are stone, so the amplified music and singing almost blasts me backwards.

In this congregation Fabio plays a major role. He sits behind the piano, a young man with a sensitive face, and 'feels' the movement of the Spirit. He plays softly when there is a time of 'waiting on the Lord', but strikes strong chords when the voices rise to declare the victory of God over all his enemies.

God called him and Marilyn, who is also a musician, from South America to be a part of his army in the land of Israel.

My father came to Argentina from Poland at the age of three. My mother was born in Argentina, but her grandparents also came from Poland. My father was a tailor.

When he arrived in Argentina, the authorities changed

his Polish name from Jelska to Jelski, which my father didn't
mind about.

I grew up in a middle-class family with a few Jewish
friends around me. With some I spoke about God. Not
only about the Jewish feasts, and so on, but about real
spiritual subjects. Even then I was searching. I felt insecure
as a boy and often afraid.

My sisters married and I remained at home alone. It didn't
make that much difference to me; it meant that there was
more space for me.

I can't say that I was happy. There was a sense of tragedy
deep in my heart which I couldn't come to grips with.

When I was seven years old my mother's mother died.
That made a deep impression on me because she lived with
us. I saw her every day and suddenly she was gone.

I often thought about death. What is death? Why are we
separated from our loved ones? I remember waking up in
the night and calling my mother. She came and sat on the
edge of my bed. I said to her, 'Mum, I don't want to die.'
And my mother said, 'Child, you're not going to die.' My
mother wasn't a believer, but those words from her lips
made a great impression on me. I began thinking about it
and wanted to know how a person could live without dying.

I read all sorts of books; philosophical and religious
books in particular interested me. I remember discussing
philosophical subjects with a friend on my twelfth birthday.

I studied the piano at the conservatoire in Buenos Aires
and wanted to be a piano teacher. When I had completed
my studies at the conservatoire, I began to get interested in
rock music, jazz and recording techniques. So I ended up
in the world of rock music, studios and recordings.

I also came into contact with drugs at a very early age. I
must have been thirteen when I had my first experience of
marijuana.

The world of music, art and drugs opened the door to
pseudo-religions for me. I came into contact with white

magic, agnosticism, the Fourth Way, Eastern mysticism, and so on. Today this is called New Age. I read all sorts of books about the different religions and cults.

And that's how I got hold of a New Testament and read the words of Jesus. In spite of my spiritual confusion, I could see that Jesus wasn't on the same level as Buddha or Muhammad. Jesus was different. He was closer to me than all the other gods. He was a sort of friend for me, but of course that wasn't possible because I was a Jew. So there was a great conflict going on inside me.

At home we celebrated the Jewish feasts like *Rosh Hashanah*, and we fasted for *Yom Kippur*, and celebrated *Pesach* with the songs and everything that goes with it. There was no place for Jesus in our house. It wasn't forbidden to speak about him, but nobody did. He was someone who didn't belong in our lives. We didn't hate Christians but there was a great distance between them and us.

I also thought that Jesus just couldn't be the Messiah, because it all seemed much too simple to me. He said, 'If you come to me, I will bring you to the Father.' That was much too easy for me. I had already read all those complicated philosophical books and so, for me, the idea that Jesus suddenly gave you eternal life when you believed in him was too childish. But deep in my heart I already had a conviction of sin. I knew that I was searching for my own justification. I wanted to attain a high level in spiritual matters so that I could please God. That's why I did all sorts of yoga exercises in order to reach the level where I could find God.

I thought that Jesus was for the poor and the ignorant. Even the word 'sin' didn't belong to this day and age, but to that of my grandmother. Do you know what I mean? That wasn't a word for my generation. Sin was something old, in which a modern person didn't believe any more.

I began experimenting with cocaine and sank even further into the depths. After that I began dealing myself. I used just enough to get high, but not too much, because I had to be able to carry out my work as a recording technician; besides which I used to play in concerts in Buenos Aires.

My powers of judgement became dulled so that I could no longer recognise the dangers. I was ruining both my body and my soul. My nervous system was affected. I drank a lot of alcohol, played rock music all night long, slept with as many girls as I wanted, and thought, 'This is freedom,' not realising that I had become a slave to sin.

In the meantime, I continued to search for truth, for God. I was never an atheist. I still believed that there was a God, even though he was far away from me. Jesus stood a little closer to me. Jesus was at least a human being; when he walked on earth, he had spoken just like me. But I couldn't accept his teachings—they were too simple.

I did a course at the School of Self Knowledge: how to strengthen your awareness. The strange thing was that there they gave me the assignment of reading through the Old and New Testaments. They said, 'There are so many mysteries, try to find out what is true.'

This course caused me to become impotent. The study affected me physically, but even more emotionally, confusing me further. I couldn't treat things superficially; I had to be conscious of who I was, twenty-four hours a day. According to my teachers, I should ask myself continually who I was as a being in relation to the universe. For example, if I took my head in my hands, I had to trace and consciously experience every muscle movement.

I had ended up in the world of death and Satan. Deep inside myself I knew that I had to put a stop to it, but I couldn't. I knew that these things couldn't be from God. But God allowed me to come to a dead end.

One evening I became angry about these doctrines and burned all my books. I had a library of mystic works, which were pretty valuable too. But I couldn't stand the strain any longer and took my books up on to the roof and burned them there. I was angry because these books had robbed me of my sex life. I hated God and everyone. My *karma* was to die far from God. I didn't know how I could get in touch with God. My Jewishness was hidden away deep in my heart. I was living in a Catholic country and felt just enough of a Jew to be unhappy but not enough of a Jew to gain strength from it.

I remembered that as a child I had heard stories of Moses, Abraham and David, and that I had been proud to belong to this divine family. But where was this divine power that had led Israel in early days? I knew that the patriarchs hadn't been ordinary leaders, but had had a special relationship with God. They received power from him to do miracles.

I had a Jewish friend, Mika, who had a recording studio in his house. We practised every week, and later we performed together. This friend read the Bible. He, a Jew, read the New Testament! He was also searching for God and we talked about it together, mostly into the early hours. Sometimes we took our Bibles and read together.

I decided to move in with him in Arribeños Street. More people came to live there, and we formed a sort of commune. They were mostly young musicians who were also searching for God. We tried to find God through the Bible. We read the Bible together without understanding much of it. We also had a sort of prayer, 'God, we believe that the Holy Scriptures come from you,' we said, 'and we ask you to show us who you are.'

We used drugs and lived in a world of confusion and spiritual chaos, but I did always have my Bible with me. I also believed that Jesus had come down to earth, but not for the Jews. My friend had a theory: 'God shows himself directly to the Jews; they don't need a mediator like Jesus. The Gentiles need Jesus.' So I paid no attention to Jesus.

The months went by. I worked hard in the recording studios, used cocaine and felt more and more miserable. The revolutionary ideas I proclaimed about art couldn't

disguise my emptiness. When I walked along the street I
saw all those people and their children, the people of the
future. They just lived to enjoy themselves. These children
would be put in the same mould as their parents, through
education and schooling, just living for themselves. I
rebelled against that. I called out, 'Let us have fun and liberate
ourselves.' But I was more of a slave than they were.

Then the opportunity came to take a trip to Israel. A
friend in Israel wrote to say that he would like to see me
once again. At that time I was practically living in the
recording studio. Sometimes I only slept for an hour a day.
I had come to the conclusion that there was only one way
to break free of the world of drugs, alcohol and sex: to leave
Argentina. Perhaps it would be good for me if I left
everything behind and went to Israel.

I played the piano, keyboards and drum machine in a
band. We performed at all sorts of concerts and turned them
into a stunning show.

Omar Zaltron, a friend of my colleague, came to watch
one of these concerts. We invited him to come and have a
drink with us in Arribeños Street afterwards. When he
entered the house, he saw the Bible lying on the kitchen
table. He asked us, 'Hey, do you read the Bible here?'

Yes, we did.

He said, 'Do you know what the Bible says about real
freedom?' And he began to explain to us how Jesus came
to accomplish his divine task and redeem the whole world.

I thought, 'This chap is crazy. He doesn't know what
he's talking about.' But there were others in the commune
who did listen to him. We asked Omar where he'd been
the past few years, and he told us that he'd been to a Bible
college and become a preacher. That was just too crazy to
be true! He had also been a drug user, and in conflict with
society, and now he himself had become a part of the
establishment.

Omar kept visiting us, and told us more and more about

Christ. He explained to us that God wanted to have a
relationship with us and wanted to give us peace. Jesus was
the perfect sacrifice, for which the Jews were waiting.

I began to listen very carefully. This was dangerous,
because if I gave in to this way of thinking, it would turn
my whole world upside down.

Slowly the idea began to take root in me that Jesus could
be the Redeemer of Israel. But if I believed that, I would
be betraying my family and my culture.

For me Jesus was in my thinking at that time only a
figure who hung on a cross in a Christian church. I could
see that there was a similarity between Judaism and
Catholicism: the emptiness of the service, the worship from
a cold heart.

Omar visited us once again and spoke with a few of the
young people who lived with us. They were so impressed
that they accepted Jesus and were baptised.

Now this 'simple way' was getting closer to me, and I
didn't want to have anything to do with it. However, I also
had a powerful realisation of how great the distance between
God and me was. But the 'simple way' of Jesus was still
too difficult for me.

Marilyn shared the room with me, and she was one of
the girls from our commune who accepted Jesus. She taught
music, was an excellent pianist and a good singer. Straight
away she was through with living with me. She couldn't
explain why. The only thing that she could say was, 'God
doesn't think it's right that we live together like this.'

I became angry and asked, 'What's not right about
me?' I thought that I had done something wrong. I didn't
understand it, but she didn't either.

Just before I left we had a farewell party, but it was rather
melancholy. We all knew something was not right with
our lifestyle—we drank a lot and went to bed with each
other. The changes were already beginning.

I left Argentina in this state, thinking about the testimonies of my close friends who had suddenly begun to believe in Jesus.

I arrived in Israel and travelled straight to Jerusalem. I walked through the streets of Zion and wept. I didn't know why. Perhaps there was a mystic spirit in Jerusalem that affected your emotions. I didn't understand why I had to weep all day.

I opened the Bible and read, 'May there be peace within your walls' (Ps 122:7). But I felt absolutely unworthy to be within these walls. I thought, 'This is God's holy mountain and I am foul and impure.' I realised that I was standing on holy ground in the city that he had built for himself. I wept when I visited David's grave and the Mount of Olives.

In the little park on Mount Sion, where strong winds have bent the trees so that they lean in the direction of the Temple Square, I sat down. It was cold, wet and windy and a procession of students passed by. Suddenly I realised that God's grace had spared my life many times.

When I lived in the world of drugs the police once raided my room to search for drugs, but I succeeded in running away through a back door. I asked myself, 'Who saved me from prison? Who is the God who holds his hands over my life?' I could not stop crying and felt: this is the crossroads of my life.

I spent all morning walking through the old city weeping. People stared at me because I was talking to myself out loud. All the time this prayer welled up from deep within, 'God, why have you brought me here? I am so unworthy to be here.'

Marilyn, this fantastic woman I had left behind in Argentina, had written to me, telling me how God was changing her life and that of my friends; how Jesus had begun to speak to them—about all the wonderful things the Holy Spirit was doing in her life. A lot had changed in that house in Arribeños Street in Buenos Aires. My friends experienced all sorts of things, with God changing their lives more and more profoundly.

They sent me a book about the Jewish Messiah and pointed out prophecies in the Old Testament which referred to Jesus. I compared these texts from the Old Testament with the New Testament and had to admit that they fitted. The pieces of the puzzle began to come together.

I moved to a kibbutz close to Jerusalem, Ramat Rachel, and went to live in a guest house and visit the *ulpan* to learn Hebrew.

But I missed my friends in Argentina more and more. I wanted to see them and to hear from them what was happening. I knew that they had something I lacked, something that I was seeking desperately. I trusted them—they wouldn't hide anything from me; they weren't hypocrites. We were used to being honest and open with each other. If they hadn't found peace and joy in God, they would tell me so honestly, because they wouldn't lie to me.

A week later—it was April 1983—I travelled to a kibbutz near Acre where relatives of mine were living. I went to the beach near Acre and saw how the sun slowly sank into the Mediterranean Sea. I sat on a rock and again read my Bible.

The Book of Romans had always been incomprehensible to me; I could never understand it, but now I read Romans 11:11, which says that God will bring salvation to the Gentiles thereby awakening jealousy in the Jews. I was jealous of my friends in Argentina. Most of them weren't Jews, but they worshipped my God, the God of Abraham, Isaac and Jacob, and they knew him better than I did.

After five months in Ramat Rachel I found a room in the house of a lesbian leader of the feminist movement that I met in the *ulpan*. Awful theories which I had to listen to were launched there and my eyes saw disgusting things every night. And I knew deep within that I wanted the same as my friends in Argentina. My whole being wanted to be born again.

I read the Bible and searched for the truth, but then again I tried to twist everything so that, untroubled, I could carry on with my sinful life. I continued to use drugs and felt powerless to make essential changes in my life.

I now really began thinking that there was no hope for me any more and that I was lost for ever. I didn't experience pleasure in drugs any more either. The parties I went to were worthless. Even in Israel you can be completely lost.

I knew that I had been born a Jew and looked for my Jewish roots. What did that mean in my life? Why did God do all those miracles for my forefathers? I became more and more aware of the fact that I was a Jew. That which was so deeply hidden in me suddenly came clearly to the surface: 'You have a responsibility. You have something to tell the world.' I didn't know then what I was going to have to tell to the world. The law was too difficult to proclaim to the world. What would my message have to be then?

I sat there alone in Jerusalem and in the greatest confusion. I had fallen out with my friend about money, and was walking through the city looking for work. Never had I been so alone.

I travelled to Eilat and went after a job: cleaning toilets in a hotel. At least I was earning something again.

I read John's Gospel, in which Jesus promises a new life to all who come to him. Jesus said that I had to be born of water and of the Spirit. That was precisely what I was longing for. I'd been looking for it half my life: to be able to begin again, to experience rebirth, to become another person. God's prophet Jesus offered the way to God.

I had lain in my bed staring at the ceiling for so many nights, saying to God, 'Why was I born Fabio? Why not Richard, Robert or whoever? Why have I been given this life, these awful disappointments and the loneliness which follows me everywhere? Why can't I be somebody different?

Why don't I get a new chance, God?' How often had I prayed like that and longed for a new start. And there it was written clearly in letters before me. Jesus said that I had to be reborn.

When I got back to Jerusalem I tried to think about these two things: the need to be reborn and being jealous of the Gentiles who had found him. But Jerusalem was lonely again. The only people I met were a couple of girls in a café and a drug dealer.

I went outside the city on the Sabbath, to sit on a mountain with a view over the whole city, and began to pray. I told God that I wanted to believe in his word. I said, 'Jesus, I know that you are the only one who can bring me to God. I accept you as Messiah. After all that reading and searching I understand that only you can save me. Your blood is the blood of reconciliation, the Jewish sacrifice to cleanse my soul. Come Messiah and change my life, because I can't satisfy the demands of God. God, help me and give me new life.'

I went back to my room and woke the next morning with the same pain in my back that I got up with every day. I still had flat feet and I felt terrible. I thought, 'Does the new life have to start like this?' I still had major financial problems too. I found work in a recording studio in Tel Aviv, but could never earn enough.

I had yet to learn that I had begun a new spiritual life, but that many other things would only change slowly. Later the Lord also gave me physical health, but he began by changing my soul and my mind. I had to learn to accept it in faith. I was like a baby and had great need of a family. A baby can't change his own nappies or feed himself either. I dirtied my soul again so easily.

But there was something which had changed. The greatest change which I myself noticed, was that I no longer had the desire to go to bars and use drugs. In the past it had even been a sort of thrill to know that I was in the places God disapproved of. But I no longer needed that.

The loneliness didn't hurt me any more. I even enjoyed it, being alone with God. I felt safe. God was with me. He sat opposite me and talked to me. The things he said touched the depths of my heart. I saw that the whole of Jerusalem was waiting for her Redeemer to return. I walked through the streets and prayed continuously, 'Come now, Lord, come now, Lord.'

I thought that I was the only Jew in the whole of Israel who believed in Jesus. That was why I spoke to everyone about what I believed. I wasn't aware that you could get into trouble by doing that. It didn't bother me either; I had to tell people that Jesus was the Messiah.

I went to visit my family in the kibbutz near Acre and told them that I had discovered that Jesus is the Messiah, and they began to laugh. I said, 'This is serious, it really is in the Bible.'

On the bus I spoke to people and told them the same thing. I would have liked to tell everyone in Israel what I had discovered.

I wasn't aware that this can mean persecution. This was so important for the future of Israel that everyone had to hear it. Some people laughed at me, others said terrible things to me, but some were interested.

As a result of my meeting with God I wanted to pay back my debts. So I took the bus to Eilat and found work in a hotel. In addition, I played in small bands here and there. After two months I had earned enough money to pay off my debts.

One day I was in the Peace Café where all the beatniks drank beer. I sat next to a young man who asked for my address. I picked up my bag and when I opened it he saw my Bible. Surprised, he asked, 'Hey, do you read the Bible?'

I said, 'Yes, I read the Bible and I believe what's written in it.'

He asked, 'Do you know Crazy John? That's the Dutchman who comes in here sometimes and speaks about Jesus. He holds quite nice meetings, with free food. You can just go there to his home on a Friday evening.' And he wrote down the address of John Pex for me.

I went back to my room in the 'Sing Sing'. That was a hostel with bars on the windows, like a prison. Everyone in Eilat called that building the 'Sing Sing'. In a sense, there were a lot of prisoners living there—people who were prisoners of sin.

I lived with a German girl there. She worked in the same hotel and was also looking for God. But she tried to find God through Eastern books, reincarnation, and so forth.

I had to meet this Crazy John and talk to him about God and Jesus. I was on fire inside as a result of all that I had experienced of God, but was full of questions about the Messiah, the Bible, the New Testament and so on. The only information that I got about God came from the letters from Argentina. But there were weeks between letters and I needed answers now, straight away.

So I left the chaos of the 'Sing Sing' behind me and went looking for Crazy John. I found the house, knocked, and a man with short blond hair and a golden beard said in a loud voice, 'Come in!' I opened the door and saw a beam of light like I'd never seen before in my life. That light was absolutely the light of the Messiah. The whole of John's family and their relationship with each other spread that light.

John is a Dutch sailor who came to Eilat to live like a hippy on the beach, found the Lord and began, with his American-Jewish wife Judy, a successful evangelistic ministry.

I went into the room, sat on a sofa and said, 'I am a Jew who has discovered that Jesus is the Messiah.'

Their mouths fell open in amazement. That didn't happen very often in Israel: someone stepping into your room and telling you that he is a Jew who believes in Jesus and wants to know more. John said, 'Begin at the beginning.'

I understood that he really wanted to know what sort of a person I was, because there are so many odd characters walking around Eilat. I told him that I really was born again, but that I still felt like a little baby and that I longed to know more.

John asked me, 'Why do you live in sin? You can't go on like that. You need a family to take you in, love you and take care of you.' He looked at Judy, his wife, for a moment and then said, 'Why don't you come and live here with us?'

I thought, 'That German girl is waiting for me in the "Sing Sing". It's already teeming with small children here. I can't come here too.' So I declined, and went back to the 'Sing Sing'. The next morning I went to work as usual.

In the evening I went to my room and put on some coffee. Suddenly it seemed as if the whole building had been turned upside-down, and I was falling downwards in a spiral. I knew that God was speaking to me. Opposite me the girl sat smoking hash. And I said to her, 'It can't go on like this. This is not the will of God.' I was convicted of my sin and felt that I should turn my back on this world. The previous day I hadn't been ready to leave, but now I hated this place.

I said to the girl, 'I'm sorry, but I'm leaving here and going to live with Crazy John, read the Bible, and so on. Perhaps I'll come back again later.'

At John's I was received as if I were a member of the family. They gave me love and care and a bed in the *succah* behind the house. I thought, 'Now take a look and see if they're still so nice to each other when you're at home with them twenty-four hours a day.' But the good atmosphere was always there, day and night. They weren't acting!

John asked me if I wanted to give up my job in order to have more time to study the Bible with him. I did.

We began each morning by praying together and then we did a Bible study. In the afternoon we went to the beach together to witness for Jesus. He also took me to my old haunt, the Peace Café, where we approached people.

One day John told me that he was going to take a trip to the Sinai to take the gospel to the Bedouin. He had made good contact with these people and I could go with him.

At the Egyptian border we had to pray really hard, because we had cassettes and Bibles with us. But the soldiers let us pass.

During the journey we drove along a beach and got out to rest for a while. Suddenly John couldn't find me anywhere. He discovered me later on the beach, where I was sitting smoking hash with a pretty girl. That happened because I still had a lot of bitterness in my heart and I didn't yet understand the meaning of the word freedom.

John took me home with him and taught me a few lessons. He didn't judge me. He didn't reject me, but explained in a factual manner that I'd done wrong, not by breaking rules and regulations, but because God wants us to take good care of our bodies. That is why it is better not to do some things, such as smoking hash with a beautiful girl on the beach during an evangelistic trip! We even laughed about it. John could tell the story so well, how he had lost me and later found me again on the beach. He could understand me very well because he'd had a background like mine.

Meetings with Messianic Jews were held in a hostel that they called The Shelter. Ja'acov Damkani came to us, and other Jewish leaders too. In The Shelter, which was situated not far from the bus station, you saw young people from all over the world talking together, eating the food they had cooked and . . . reading their Bibles in a totally relaxed atmosphere. That was precisely what I needed.

I needed people around me. Free people. People who walked around the house barefoot in the heat of the day and went to the beach in the afternoon. It was a fantastic time. I enjoyed the Bible studies in the morning, evangelising on the beach in the afternoons and the meetings with other believers in the evenings.

But I didn't want to stay in Israel for ever. This unrest drove me to pack my things and go on a trip. I wanted to travel via Greece through Europe to Holland. I knew another musician who was at the school of music in Maastricht and I wanted to visit him. In addition, I had got to know Bram and Marieke, a fine believing Dutch couple. And Els, a hippy who had slept on the beach of Eilat and used drugs; she too had come to faith.

I looked them up in Holland and they introduced me to Christian heavy rock bands. So I attended various gospel concerts. It was good for my spiritual growth to see people with my background coming to the Lord. In my own way I witnessed to the power of God that had changed my life.

But I longed for South America more and more. So when I had visited Holland, Belgium and Germany, I took a plane to Brazil and travelled on from there.

Mika came all the way from Argentina, a distance of 2,000 kilometres, on his motorbike to pick me up. We were so happy to see each other again. He had become a different person; so had I. Mika had grown in the Lord.

Back in Buenos Aires we went to live in a house in Tronador Street, but everything was totally different now. I now gave Bible studies to young people! We formed a house church which evangelised among the musicians and drug addicts. We now praised God with our music.

And I met Marilyn again, the girl I had lived with earlier. It took some time before we got used to the fact that we were both new people. A new Marilyn stood before me. A Marilyn who was filled with the Holy Spirit. She had once stood in her room and the Holy Spirit came upon her. She cried and began to speak in tongues.

I did not believe in these things. But very tenderly she sat beside me, laid her hands on my head and prayed for

me that the Lord would fill me too with his Spirit. At that
moment something broke deep within me, and then a kind
of fire welled up from within. First I started to cry, then I
prayed, and then I could not stop the new language of the
Spirit flowing over my lips. The first thing I said was, 'Now
I see!' I really could see clearly now.

I was a totally different Fabio. Now our love for
each other returned and we decided to marry officially.
Our wedding was sealed with the birth of our first son,
Jeremias.

A young couple, Adriana and Raoul, came to the house
church. They too are in Haifa now. We had already known
each other for thirteen years because we grew up in the
same place.

Marilyn kept mentioning with increasing frequency that
we had to leave. There was some tension in the house church
about dogmas, and so on, but God uses everything to bring
Jews to Israel—sometimes persecution, sometimes political
problems. You don't always realise it, but God is busy for
a long time beforehand, making preparations to bring about
a change in your life's path. When I arrived in Argentina,
I told everyone, 'I'm staying here five years at the most.'
And precisely four and a half years later, we left. I was
homesick for Eilat and for Israel. I read the letters which
I'd written over and over again.

I asked the minister where I should go because my wife
was Italian and wanted to travel to Rome where her sister
lives, but we also thought about Switzerland where my
sister lives, and . . . Australia! My minister said, 'Go where
the door is wide open. You have always been a man who
kicks against everything. Stop trying to force things for
once. Let God lead you in peace. Give everything over to
him.'

You can't imagine how many miracles began to happen
then. When I decided to go to Israel, everything went
smoothly. We arrived in Beersheba and got a place in the

absorption centre, where we studied Hebrew for a year. We received immigrant status.

Beersheba was exactly midway between Safad, where my parents lived, and Eilat, where my friends were. I could easily attend the meetings now.

Marilyn was pregnant again and as a seal on our new life in Israel, Joel was born. I realised that I now had the responsibility for a wife and two babies. I didn't want to shirk my responsibility like a hippy any more. I lay awake at night because of it. During the day I hardly spoke to anyone; the situation became tense. Satan whispered to me to leave Israel. He doesn't like the fact that more and more Messianic Jews are living here.

Then the leaders of the Elijah Church in Haifa asked if I would be in charge of the praise and worship and start a coffee bar for the youngsters. In addition, I could help with the maintenance of the buildings. They offered me a house and a salary.

All our major steps in the Lord have been sealed with the birth of another child. When we left Tronador Street, Marilyn was expecting Jeremias, when we moved to Israel she was expecting Joel, and when we moved to Haifa she was expecting Dafna as a seal from the Lord of our new life.

But first I had to do military service. And the Lord used this time to change my heart. I saw that it was God's intention for me to be a real Israeli in everything, to learn the language well and to speak about finding the Messiah. Now I work in a rehabilitation centre for drug addicts and other street people.

I felt more of a Jew once I'd got to know the Messiah. Judaism wasn't a dead religion for me any more with all sorts of customs and feasts. I saw that God's plan for the world will be completed by our people.

Jesus made me more Jewish, absolutely. Before I met him, I was a poor imitation of what a Jew should be. I have now become a real son of Abraham. But I can also have a lot of love for the Gentiles because the dividing wall has been broken down by Jesus.

Jews have the special task of carrying the ark into the world—the ark in which the bread of life lies, the heavenly manna, that is, Yeshua.

It is my task to be a living sacrifice in the living temple and to carry God's word into the world. Everything awaits that.

The coming of the Messiah is near and one day he will say, 'Fabio, come home with me.' And then this Jew will go with him because he has been expecting him for a long time.

12
Olga, the Young Woman from Russia

I met Olga Sollertinskaya for the first time in Holland. She stayed with friends who had brought her there to help with a television production.

She lived then in Leningrad, now St Petersburg. I remember Leningrad: the Hermitage, the former palace from the golden age of Czar Peter; the wide boulevards and statues dating back to its maritime past.

From this same city came this young Jewish woman. Her life changed when she was touched in a powerful way by *Ruach Hakodesh*. She became free to be herself, two years before she made the *Aliyah*. Olga's forefathers were once led out of slavery in Egypt and entered the Promised Land, Eretz Israel. This exodus is being repeated at the moment. Hundreds of thousands of Jews from all the East European countries are being led to Israel.

The parallel between the earlier exodus and Olga's experience is based on the Bible. Through Jeremiah God said:

However, the days are coming . . . when men will no longer say, 'As surely as the Lord lives, who brought the Israelites

209

up out of Egypt,' but they will say, 'As surely as the Lord lives, who brought the Israelites up out of the land of the north and out of all the countries where he had banished them.' For I will restore them to the land I gave to their forefathers. 'But now I will send for many fishermen,' declares the Lord, 'and they will catch them. After that I will send for many hunters, and they will hunt them down on every mountain and hill . . .' (Jer 16:14–16).

God said through Isaiah: 'I will say to the north, "Give them up!" and to the south, "Do not hold them back"' (Is 43:6).

Every exodus creates pain and troubles. So it was in the days of Moses and so it is in these modern times. Thousands of Soviet Jews have put up a struggle against the Russian bureaucracy and waited months for an exit visa.

I met Olga just before she was going to give in her application forms to the emigration office. She had no idea how to get through all the problems of dealing with the emigration process and did not know where the money would come from for plane tickets and all other expenses. But she trusted in God.

Right before our eyes we see the fulfilment of centuries-old prophecies. At first a few dozen came, then hundreds, and, after that, thousands per day. The 'fishermen' are busy fishing out the Jews in the 'lands of the north', but according to the prophecy 'hunters' will also come, who will drive the Jews back home. These developments will ultimately bring us a step closer to the coming again of the Messiah and the 'restoration of all things' (Acts 3:21). In Olga the second exodus is embodied.

It wasn't easy to come to Holland. I am here now for the television documentary *USSR Goodbye*. In it we follow a Jewish family who emigrate to Israel from Russia. Despite the great changes that have already taken place, you still have to fight for months to get a visa. But still, a few years ago it was much more complicated.

In Russia it is possible to submit only one application at a time for a trip abroad, so I cannot submit my request to emigrate to Israel before my return from this trip. I hope that it won't take too long. Some of my friends have been waiting for years.

When I have my visa, I'll take a flight from Moscow to Budapest or Prague and then a charter flight to Tel Aviv, and then I am home! The land of Israel! That's the only route I can afford. There has been talk of a direct flight from Leningrad to Tel Aviv, but the Israeli consulate still can't say anything definite about it.

I am a librarian-bibliographer. I classify books in a scientific manner. I have learned to classify a book according to content, title, format, printer, date and other important data.

My father and mother are both engineers. I have a sister who emigrated to Israel in June of the year 1990.

As a teenager I used to believe in God, but I didn't know who he was. He lived somewhere up there. I supposed God to be a man who sat somewhere above us and looked down on us. He had created everything and knew everything about everybody. He led things and people, but I couldn't imagine that I could have contact with him personally. To me he was an abstract figure.

God was never spoken about at home either, and is not even now. I am the only one at home who is taken up with this.

My father has an even personality. He is a calm person who thinks deeply. We have a good relationship with each other. He doesn't understand about my religious experiences, but his attitude is respectful. What is very important to me is that he doesn't put me down.

We belong to the Jewish community in Leningrad. I have Jewish uncles, aunts and cousins. But we weren't isolated; I also had many Russian friends. In our home, everyone was welcome.

But we were not Jewish in our beliefs, at least not consciously. That is normal in Russia. In atheistic Russia there was no place for people who practise their faith. Now, thank God, it is starting to be possible. Not so long ago, people who did have a faith were still put in prison. So my parents and my friends, and all the people around me, were not religious. For them, God and religion were very far away.

We were a warm, close family. We were also very interested in art and culture. Very often we went to the Philharmonic Society to listen to good concerts, and visited theatres and museums. Sometimes it was tricky to get tickets for the good concerts. Directly or indirectly, this quest always occupied us and most of the time we succeeded. Once in the concert hall, one would see Jewish faces all around.

There was persecution in the sense that most of the Jewish families were thwarted when investigating the possibilities of further education and in getting good jobs. When my sister wanted to go to the university, the director of the university warned my grandmother, who was a doctor of psychology and teaching and holder of the chair of psychology in the Education Institute, that it would be wiser to abandon this attempt. As a Jew she would never be admitted, so it would be better for her not to try.

When I graduated from secondary school I did not attempt to enter university either, for the same reason. So I went to study at the Leningrad Institute of Culture, a different establishment with a slightly lower status than the university.

When I was fourteen and at secondary school, children from our school were planning to make a trip abroad. That would be something special. We had an exchange agreement with a school in Hungary. Children from there would come to Leningrad for two weeks, and we would go to their country.

All the preparations had been made for the trip, it was all paid for too, but suddenly a teacher said that I couldn't go with them. She was a young teacher, with whom I got on well, and I noticed that she found it difficult to say this. She took me aside and explained it to me. She said, 'It is our fault, we should have told your parents first, but since we didn't, I have to tell you now that you can't go with us.'

I asked, 'Why? Everything is all ready, and I've always had good marks.'

Finally she told me why: 'What nationality is written in your passport, Olga?'

I said, 'Jewish.'

Then she said, 'That's it, that's the reason why you can't come with us.'

That was hard to swallow, especially when there was a boy who didn't do very well but came from a socialist working-class family and he was allowed to go to Hungary instead of me. You learn to live with it, but sometimes it hurts. So, in a negative way, I was reminded of the fact that I was a Jew.

When we came together with friends, parents of friends and cousins on the Sabbath or a feast day, we would sit around the table and the conversation was always about children who were having difficulty in getting into the university or who couldn't find work because of their being Jewish.

Later on, when I graduated from the Institute, I had the same experiences. It was difficult to find interesting jobs. I finished a three-year course as an English-speaking guide. I tried to find work in which I could use my knowledge of English.

I was sixteen years old when I told my parents that I wanted to go to the main synagogue. It was autumn and *Simchat Torah*. The celebrations don't have any great religious significance for most of the Soviet Jews. Participation is more a question of cultural background. You can meet friends whom you haven't seen for months. There are so many Jews around that you get the feeling that we are still a nation.

But in front of the synagogue is a tall, modern building with large windows and at that time agents from the police would sit there with cameras to photograph all the people who go into the synagogue. A cousin of mine had once got into difficulties as a result of this. So when I had to go to the synagogue I tried to be very careful.

I wanted to go to the synagogue, because I had an increasing desire to experience God. That was why I also wanted to learn Hebrew. But that was too dangerous then and my parents always stopped me.

When I finished secondary school I had the desire to enter the Academy of Art. That was a shock for my parents who were quite adjusted to the idea of my studying at the Institute. I already painted a little, but nothing that my parents could appreciate. But my attempt was a failure and so as not to miss a year I took a secretarial course. I learned to type faster than I could write and got my diploma with honours.

For three years I worked at the scientific research institute and after that I found freelance work with a co-operative. I could work from home for as many hours as I wanted and that suited me fine.

When I was nineteen I got married. But the relationship with my husband lasted only three years and then we separated. As a result of our relationship I gave birth to a beautiful daughter. When she was two years old she asked, 'Mummy, why don't I have a daddy?' I explained to her that it is possible to have two parents, or just a mummy or a daddy. 'But,' I said, 'perhaps Mummy will meet a man one day whom we both love and you will have a daddy.' She was satisfied with this explanation and went and told everyone, 'Do you know what? We're looking for a daddy . . . .' She is now seven years old and a beautiful child whom I love very much. She is happy with the situation as it is now.

Judaism interested me, but then again it didn't. I found a religion that emphasised laws more than relationships extremely difficult. I found that to be abnormal and unnatural. I imagined God as somebody or something alive. A relationship with him must be built on the heart's feelings, not on proclaimed rules and laws.

I understood that the deep satisfaction I was looking for wasn't to be found in Judaism as it was expressed in Russia. Then I began getting interested in Eastern mysticism. But after a while the religious side of it didn't fulfil me. I was only interested in the philosophical aspects.

In the summer of 1989 I went to a farewell party. A friend of mine was emigrating to the United States. The farewell party was held in his house and there I met a nice girl. She was a Jewish girl and we liked each other. She was conspicuous because of her beauty. I couldn't keep my eyes off of her—she was strikingly beautiful. It was as though she was shining.

We began to talk to each other and this girl told me that she had had a meeting with God a few months ago. It was the glory of God that I had seen on her. She made me jealous. The girl told me about an evangelical Russian-Finnish church, forty minutes by train outside Leningrad. She had met the Lord there and it was there that her life had been so radically changed.

The following day was a Sunday, and she invited me to go to the church. I agreed immediately, because I felt there was something very special about the way we met. So I visited that church and was very impressed. At once I felt in my heart, 'This is what I've been longing for. Here is what I've been searching for all these years.' A feeling of happiness flowed through me.

I was especially impressed by the atmosphere. This wasn't 'religious'. I had always thought that a certain pious, restrained atmosphere pervaded churches, but here people laughed, there was singing and God was praised. People sang songs easily and happily, accompanied by all sorts of musical instruments. The minister spoke in normal, simple language. This was what I was looking for. I went again the following Sunday.

My new friend was full of life. I am more reserved. If a matter is important then it has to be deeply and seriously thought through. I don't live by my intellect, but from my heart, my soul. I am subject to moods and didn't think it good to make a quick decision. I wanted to make a deliberate, well-considered decision before I yielded myself to the Lord. I didn't want to be impulsive, like many others are.

When we went to the meetings, people tried to push me to go forward to talk with the preacher or let him pray for me personally. But I said again, 'Wait, I am not ready yet.'

I saw other people become affected by the service and go forward when the preacher invited, 'Come, if you need prayer.' But my conviction is that you have to be ready deep down inside to take such a step, otherwise there's no point. You should realise what an important decision you are about to make, otherwise you will not have deep roots and you will bear no fruit.

I was made ready by God himself. My heavenly Father prepared me for this decision. I began to read the Bible and the New Testament and believed everything very naturally. I believed what I read and began to believe in Jesus with all my heart.

Four months later, something happened. It was on a

Sunday, and I was alone at home in my flat. My daughter was playing at my parents' house, in the garden. It was cosy and peaceful in the kitchen. I sat down and began to read my Bible. And suddenly something unbelievable happened. It was like a revelation. I could see what I was reading. I felt the Lord come and stand next to me and a wave of great joy swept over me. I was filled with an inner joy. I had to laugh and cry at the same time, and suddenly I began praying in another language. It was a miracle! I was so surprised; it flooded straight from my heart, so beautiful, so happy. I had to cry, laugh, pray and sing all at the same time. It was an unbelievable celebration with the Lord. It lasted for about four hours. I couldn't do anything but cry, laugh, pray and sing.

When I called my friend, at first I could only cry. Surprised, she asked, 'What's the matter with you? Your voice sounds so strange.'

I said, 'It is so difficult to describe. You know that it says in the Bible that Elijah was translated? That's how I feel now.'

It was hours before everything became normal again. I was so glad that God allowed me to come to him in a way I could handle, a way that suited my personality; that he didn't force me, but slowly prepared me for it.

This was so important because it brought into my relationship with God the feeling of deep trust and love. That helped me a lot in my growth as his child. It helped me overcome some difficulties with relationships in that church and some problems at home.

Another blessing for me was meeting believers from Holland, who later became my special friends. Through them, I discovered new things. Their attitude in particular made an impression on me. They spoke differently about God. For them, God was a Father. A Father who embraces you when you're sad and forgives you when you've done something wrong. They taught me to live by faith and to

expect everything from the Lord, right down to the tiniest
detail.

Through them the Father told me how to develop a deep
relationship with him and my life definitely changed. I said,
'Father, I don't want anything for myself any more. I want
to give all my own thoughts, feelings and plans to you.
You gave me this new life, you will take care of me. I am
your child. I want your thoughts and your feelings in my
heart.'

In the eyes of my family and friends it was madness to
end all my self-interest, but I felt from within that I had to
take that step. In my new life I didn't want to trust in people,
but in God.

I can't say that it was very easy, especially as far as special
contacts were concerned, for in Russia you can hardly get
anywhere through official channels. Whether it's food, a
job, education, or tickets for a concert, everything works
via connections. And I had an extensive network of connections, and had many friends. I knew musicians and artists
and went to exhibitions and concerts. But that life no longer
satisfied me. When I see how I have changed over this past
year, I can hardly recognise myself any more. I react
differently to the things I come up against. I now take
decisions with him, because he knows what suits my
character best.

I talk with the Father about the things which touch me
deepest. I talk about my needs with Jesus, like I would with
an older brother. Sometimes I only say to the Father that I
love him. He is my loving Father. Sometimes I look up
and just say, 'Father I love you; thank you that you care for
me.'

If I need to cry, or if I am happy, he is with me and sees
and knows me. Sometimes I only whisper, 'Thank you,
Father.' It is a wonderful feeling to have such a relationship
with the Almighty.

My Father also began to reveal to me more of my

background. I started to understand that God had begun with the Jews in the Old Testament, that Jesus addressed himself to the Jews. But Jesus felt great sorrow because his own people would not believe in him. Everything that he and the Father had prepared was first for his chosen people, but they didn't want to receive it.

That will change in the future; the situation is already beginning to change. God is removing the veil from their hearts so that they can see who Yeshua is. The time has now come when many Soviet Jews are emigrating. This is a special time for God the Father. He is gathering his people back into his land.

First the Jews will come back to Israel, then God will give them 'a new heart' (Ezek 36:26).

Now I understand why I have not emigrated to the United States of America, even though during the last six years I have had several chances to go there. But my parents objected because it could endanger their jobs.

Now, since I am a believer, I want to live only in Israel and nowhere else. I want to go home. Israel is the only country on earth where I won't be a foreigner. We have been immigrants in Russia for centuries. Many things are forbidden to us. There have always been difficulties. The political situation is uncertain and tense. But I want to return 'home'. The Father will lead me and take care of me.

God has given me work. I was chosen to help with the production of a film for television about a modern *Aliyah*. So many miracles happened during the preparation time. I had to find a family that we could follow and film from Leningrad to Tel Aviv. I found interesting families, but they still weren't the people that God had intended for this. After three months of searching I still hadn't found the right family.

One day I spoke to my sister who was also getting everything ready to emigrate. She had the greatest difficulty in getting tickets and a visa. You have to stand in a queue every morning for weeks. Every day you have to go to the emigration office again to sign your name. My sister was number 7,600 when she first went. There were 7,599 people ahead of her in the queue.

We talked about these problems. I told her that I had asked all my friends if they knew of a family that was suitable for the television documentary, but that no one knew of anyone. And the filming would soon have to start.

'Oh,' said my sister, 'I met a family at the emigration office today; they were such nice intelligent people. They might be right for you.'

I said, 'Who are they?' And she gave me the telephone number of Leonid and Xenne Landa.

I called them and told them that I was looking for a family with children for a film about a modern *Aliyah*. They discussed it briefly with each other and then said, 'Yes, we agree to do it.'

I knew immediately that this was from God. They turned out to be two engineers with three nice children. They weren't religious Jews, but on their journey to Israel they began to realise more and more that they were being led. The woman in the reception centre in Budapest said so too. She saw all these people with their baggage; old men and women with lined faces and young people with children. They had come together from all the countries of Eastern Europe. A great migration of a nation. They had tears in their eyes.

I am glad that God used me to help with this beautiful film that has touched many people. It is a piece of human drama that has to do with God's plan for the world.

God gave me another job. I was privileged to organise the concert tour of the Dutch classical ensemble 'New Wine' in the Soviet Union. They sing songs of consolation for Israel. The time I spent with these musicians was really blessed. I felt through their music that the Father spoke to me in a special and new way. He called me a 'daughter of Zion'. I begin to realise more and more the importance of this.

God has not only given me everything I needed, but especially he has given himself. He has changed me, and opened me up to myself. Now I am beginning to learn what love, trust, faith and responsibility are. And I yearn to learn how to live this new kind of beautiful life.

I believe that Jews and Christians should be united. We are saved together. We are members of one family. We are on the way to Zion together. One day we will sing songs in Jerusalem together.

'*L'shanah   haba'ah   b'irushalayim,*'—next   year   in Jerusalem!

Olga landed at Ben Gurion Airport in Israel on 2nd January 1991.

13
Messianic Jews in Europe

Helen Shapiro

Back from Israel in my search for Jews who have found the Messiah, I began to look around my own country. Would there be some Messianic Jews here? First I discovered a group in the small town of Alphen aan de Rijn, not far from the Hague. We were told to first contact a lady, Rebecca de Graaf, for these Jews want to be with their own people.

We were allowed to attend their monthly gathering. In a church meeting room we found a group of fifty people listening to an address, followed by the *Kiddush* celebrated with a small cup of wine and the singing of a few songs.

Rebecca de Graaf proved to be the Yiddish *memme* of the Dutch Messianic Jews. She is eighty-three years of age and sat up at the front in a folding chair and kept an eye on everything that happened. She thanked the ladies for baking the *oliebollen* (a typical Dutch treat during *Chanukah*), and gave an invitation for *Pesach* to the Jews, but 'believers from the nations' were told to ask permission first. In spite of her age, and some physical problems ('everything is eighty-three years old, you know') her mind is still crystal clear. She reminded me very much of Corrie ten Boom in the later years of her life.

Later on we visited 'Tante' Rebecca in her flat and she told us her life story.

She was born in the Hague in 1907. Her father was a goldsmith. She attended the Orthodox synagogue, where men and women are seated separately. Gifted in music, she was trained as a professional pianist.

She frequently visited the home of a Christian girl friend where the Bible was read after dinner. But she could not eat dinner with them, because it was not kosher. When she helped out in the friend's fashion shop she saw a Bible. Although the New Testament was a forbidden book to her, she opened it and read the words of Jesus:

> You diligently study the Scriptures because you think that
> by them you possess eternal life. These are the Scriptures that
> testify about me, yet you refuse to come to me to have life
> (Jn 5:39).

With those words the search for answers to questions such as, 'Who is Yeshua? Is he the Messiah?' had begun. The Bible convinced her that Jesus was the Messiah. When she was baptised, she went to a Christian Bible school and bombarded the teachers with questions.

In her view, the 'Christian Japheth squatted in the tent of Shem', referring to Genesis 9:27. Shem is Israel and in Japheth she sees the believers from the nations. But Japheth was not satisfied taking a minor place in Shem's tent; like a cuckoo's young he took over the place. Japheth even said that Shem no longer had a place in God's tent. But God was pleased to select Israel out of all the nations and let Yeshua be born through her. As Paul writes, 'Did God reject his people? By no means!' (Rom 11:1), and, 'God's gifts and his callings are irrevocable' (v 29).

'Tante' Rebecca told us how she married a Christian banker from Alphen aan de Rijn and was saved during the war by the miraculous hand of God. After the war her testimony was heard louder and louder and a group of Messianic Jews was formed. Most of these Jews had belonged to all kinds of churches, where they sometimes felt out of place. But here they were 'home' among believers who could understand their special need and confirm their identity as Jews who believe in Jesus.

In Eilat, the southernmost point of Israel, John and Judy Pex gave me the address of a Messianic rabbi in London. I also heard about the famous British singer Helen Shapiro, who was Messianic. I went to see for myself.

London in autumn is a dismal place. I found myself in old subways with a view of bundles of cables fastened with rusty nails to concrete walls. After changing trains I arrived at the right station, somewhere on the outskirts of town. I walked half an hour with my finger on the map and found a white wooden church: Bridge Lane Chapel.

When I entered I knew immediately that I was in the right place. I saw a man who was wearing a *kippah*.

In the middle of a group of people stood a man busily shaking hands, talking to people on his left and right, striking shoulders and smiling. He had a black beard, and joyous eyes. He was the man I was looking for, 'Rabbi' Chuck Snow. He greeted me with a broad 'Sabbath Shalom!', showed me to a seat and handed me a small book with songs and prayers for the beginning of the Sabbath.

Chuck opened the service by playing the guitar, accompanied by some other instruments. He was obviously a musician. The songs had a distinctive Jewish flavour, lots of 'Lai,lai,lais' and changes of rhythm.

There was freedom in the Spirit. A song could end in

spontaneous applause or singing in the Spirit. Half of the congregation of 120 were Jews, the other half Christians 'with a love for the Jews'.

The notices revealed the life of the congregation: Hebrew classes on Tuesday. A *mikvah* service has been arranged (in the floor of the chapel is a baptistry). Bring your friends for *Chanukah*. And so on.

As a part of the sermon, Chuck read the portion from the *Torah* for this Sabbath—Genesis 27: the story of Isaac, who steals the blessing from his brother Esau. He dealt with the hot question of the election of Israel.

Chuck warned, 'Be careful, for a wrong interpretation of this text can lead to anti-Semitism. Jacob got his birthright honestly. He bought it from his brother. Even when he was still in Rebecca's womb the two boys clashed and God said, "The older will serve the younger." God is sovereign and works out his plans even in spite of human weakness. And don't forget that at Peniel the deceiver, Jacob, became the prince, Israel.'

The next day I used the London underground once more, to have a personal interview with Chuck and his wife in their small family home. I saw the remains of a *succah* in the garden. Ruth brought me some of her booklets. One is a 'Messianic Haggadah'. She hopes to finish her studies at the university with a doctoral thesis on 'Messianic Jews since 1976'.

When I asked Chuck how he can use the title of 'rabbi' he explained that a group of sixty-five Messianic congregations in the United States came together to form the Alliance of Messianic Congregations and Synagogues. A steering committee was formed (of which Chuck is a member) for the ordination of rabbis and pastors, who can then officially carry that title.

Most of these congregations are in the United States, but some are in the United Kingdom (London and Manchester, with a few smaller groups in other towns), France, Australia and South America.

Chuck and Ruth were called from a large Messianic congregation in San Francisco to London to take over the leadership of a Messianic congregation. They are full of hope about the future. In Europe there is still so much to do. They want to give the Messianic Jews a voice and confirm their identity. They conducted an international Messianic conference, 'Yeshua 1991', in Nottingham, England, with more than 400 participants, and expect more visitors from all over Europe in the forthcoming years.

During our 'goodbyes' Ruth handed me a press release about one of their members, the singer Helen Shapiro. Her testimony is heard all over the United Kingdom and is used by God to show how it is possible that one can be Jewish and believe in Jesus.

Helen soared into international stardom at the age of fourteen. In 1963 she used the Beatles in a supporting role! She has been performing for thirty years as a jazz singer. Although Helen was raised in Judaism and always believed in God, she came to believe that Yeshua is the Messiah.

This is Helen's story:

I became interested in Buddhism, spiritualism, psychic phenomena, and so on, and I suppose for a while this satisfied me.

At the age of forty I became increasingly aware of the fact that my career had become too important in my life. I became very depressed as it seemed everything was meaningless. Bob Cranham, my music director, and his wife Pennie were Christians and Bob's faith impressed me. I was envious of him. One night, at my lowest ebb, I said, 'Okay, Jesus. If you're so great, do something. Help me!'

I had just returned from Germany when Bob put the

book *Betrayed* by Stan Telchin in my hand, saying it might be of interest to me. The next day I sat and read it all the way through. The impression it made on me was enormous. I read it again and realised how little I knew about biblical prophecy and Jewish history.

So I went out and bought a Bible and started to read. When I turned to the New Testament I was impressed how Jewish it was! The genealogy of Jesus in Matthew came as a complete surprise. I carried on as I read about this Jew Jesus and what he said and did. I was constantly turning back to the Old Testament to see how and where the prophecies were being fulfilled.

After a couple of days I decided to get an English translation of the *Tenach*, the Hebrew Scriptures. I wanted to compare this with the Christian Bible in case I was being misled. I sat at home for two and a half months with two Bibles reading and cross-referencing and devouring all this new knowledge until eventually I realised that there was no way to deny the truth of it. Jesus was the Jewish Messiah.

I went to Bob and Pennie and told them I was on the verge of becoming a believer. For hours I asked them question after question.

That night, 26th August 1987, around 10.30 pm, I asked Yeshua to come into my life and committed myself to him. There were no shooting stars, no revelations, no visitations, just a knowledge that it was right.

About a week later, that commitment went from my head to my heart, when I was worshipping. The Spirit of God came upon me and I was in tears of joy and love for my Lord.

At the same time he gave me a burden for my own Jewish people and the land of Israel. I'm starting now to assemble Messianic songs to sing for him. He gave me a talent, which I always used for myself, and now I want to use it for his glory. It is exciting to live in these times when God is pouring out his Spirit on his ancient Jewish people and it's my wish to serve him, no matter what difficulties or hardships this may entail.

When I returned to the continent, I went to France to look for Messianic friends there. In Paris I took the underground and found the Centre Messianique at de Rue Omer-Talon. Here we met the leaders of the Messianic movement in France and Belgium, Anya and Paul Ghennassia.

Paul told me how he found the Messiah.

I am a Sephardic Jew from Algeria. I was raised in a traditional Jewish family and went to the synagogue, did my *Bar Mitzvah* and all the religious tasks.

The general idea about Christians was that they have done bad things to us throughout history. Once, a young Catholic lady, who was working as a window-dresser, said to me, 'You Jews have crucified Jesus.' I decided that I did not want to have anything to do with Christians.

But God reached me, by healing my wife. My wife urged me to take her to a meeting where prayer was offered for the sick. She was healed of a tumour. After that meeting a lady offered me a Bible. I refused and said, 'Madam, I am a Jew.' Her reply was, 'Sir, it is precisely because you are a Jew that I offer you this Bible. The Bible is first for the Jew and then for the Gentile. The Jews have given us the Bible.'

I accepted that Bible and began to read, and for the first time in my life I knelt by my bed and said to the Lord, 'My God, reveal to me, show me, who Jesus is. If he is the Messiah, I will accept him, but if he is not the one promised, I don't want anything to do with it.'

I opened the Bible and read, 'He was despised and rejected by men, a man of sorrows, and familiar with suffering. . . . Surely he took up our infirmities and carried our sorrows'

(Is 53:3–5). I was overwhelmed. At that moment my wife had a Christian visitor. I ran out of my room and cried, 'Listen. God has just shown me that Jesus is really the Messiah.' Some days later I received a call from God indicating that he wanted to use me to reach my own people.

In 1964 I went to Paris and began to work among the 450,000 Jews that live there. There are more Jews in Paris than in Jerusalem! I published a magazine, *Témoignage Messianique au Peuple d'Israel* and I began to transmit radio programmes via Radio Luxembourg. One by one friends joined me. I got the feeling that I was not the only one of the remnant of Israel.

When my first wife died, I met Anya, from Finland. She worked among the Jews in Brussels, the capital of Belgium. After our wedding we started to work together. Half of the week we are in Brussels, where we lead a congregation of Messianic Jews, and the other half in Paris.

Sometimes we have an outreach on Place Pompidu in the heart of Paris. All our members wear T-shirts with the sign of a menorah, and the Hebrew letters of 'Yeshua' on the arms. On two occasions Orthodox Jews have come to disturb our street meeting and a minor riot has broken out. Some have been wounded.

There are Jewish prayer groups in several cities of France: Marseilles, Strasbourg, and some other towns. But the only Messianic congregation is here in Paris, with 110 members.

I asked Anya about the situation in Scandinavia, where she is from. Especially in Finland, there is enormous support for Israel by Christians. But also, small groups of Messianic Jews come together in the capitals of the Scandinavian countries, Helsinki, Copenhagen and Stockholm.

Now it was time for Germany. I made contact with Arie
Ben Israel, a Messianic Jew I had met before. There are no
Messianic groups in Germany, but the Voice of Reconciliation (Ruf zur Versöhnung) of Arie Ben Israel is well known
all over the German-speaking world. Arie has a special call
to speak about repentance, forgiveness and reconciliation.

Arie met God in this way:

My mother lost her first husband in the concentration camp
where she spent four terrible years. My father escaped certain
death in Auschwitz by jumping from the freight train,
crammed with Jewish people, while it was passing through
a wood.

They made their way to Russia where they survived
sixteen years of forced labour in Siberia, living on the hope
that one day they could emigrate to Israel. I was born in
1950 in difficult circumstances in Kazakstan. In 1957 the
family travelled to Poland, where the chance of emigrating
to Israel was better.

I was ten years old when I came to Israel. We were very
happy—at last we had arrived home.

One year before my *Bar Mitzvah*, my father thought it
was time to tell me his great secret. He told me that Jesus
Christ is the Jewish King and the long awaited Messiah.
This created great confusion within me, for my father was
a beloved member of the Jewish congregation. My grandfather was an Orthodox rabbi. In my opinion, Yeshua was
the great enemy of our people. In his name untold suffering
had come upon us. At my *Bar Mitzvah* my father gave me
my first New Testament. One year later he died in my
arms, praising the Lord as the King of Israel and the
Redeemer of the world.

It took me eleven years to stop resisting him. In 1972 I
had my first heart attack and after hospitalisation the doctors
told me that I had probably only five years to live.

The murder of my best friend in the 1972 Olympic Games

in Munich made me more desperate to look for the answers to my life. I had to go to Germany. In 1973 I saw Dachau. Standing in front of the crematorium I remembered the words of my father, 'We have a merciful God.' But where was his mercy that could have saved us from these horrors?

I decided to return to Israel and start a religious family. When I came back to Israel I married a *sabra*, but she insisted on a honeymoon to Munich, Germany.

On a street in inner-city Munich we heard a group of young Christians singing about Jesus. I thought, 'What a good opportunity to tell them about the horrible things they did to my people!' But a young girl from the group had the courage to come to me and simply say, 'Jesus loves you.'

I spat on the ground in front of her feet and poured out a flood of accusations over her. The girl said, 'Yes, I and my forefathers are guilty.' She asked me to forgive her and her forefathers and added, 'You can curse me, say bad things to me, even hit me and kill me—Jesus will still love you.' These words made a bomb explode in my heart. She hit me in my deepest soul. For the first time in my life, I, the arrogant Israeli, was knocked out, and that through a German girl!

The following days I wandered through the streets of Munich and bought a Bible. Back in the apartment, while my wife was out shopping, I opened the New Testament and read Matthew 2:2, 'Where is the one who has been born king of the Jews?' And at that moment the Holy Spirit came over me and convinced me that my father was right, that Yeshua is the Messiah.

My wife told me to make a choice: Jesus, or her. I could not compromise. So we flew back to Israel to divorce.

God brought me back to Germany and opened churches and groups where I could speak about forgiveness and reconciliation between Germans and Jews. On the fiftieth anniversary of the day on which Hitler made the law reducing Jews to second-rate citizens, the start of the holocaust, I led a silent march for repentance in the town of Nuremberg. Ten thousand men and women from twenty-two nations and many different churches came to Nuremberg. I spoke from the same platform on which Hitler once stood, and prayed aloud a prayer of repentance and asked God to forgive the Germans. We also held a conference in Berlin in 1988 on the same subject: to pray for forgiveness and reconciliation.

I, as a Messianic Jew from Israel, represent all the Jews that have suffered through the Nazis and offer forgiveness in Yeshua's name.

After Germany, my last appointment was in Amsterdam. My search in Israel and Europe was almost finished. I was overwhelmed by what I had heard and seen. The stories I had heard were so full of God's Spirit. Many times I listened to them with tears in my eyes. I felt privileged to meet these 'firstfruits'; to see the 'first drops of the latter rain'.

A new Messianic congregation had sprung up in Amsterdam, under the leadership of a Jewish army chaplain, Leon Erwteman, and his wife Elze. This Messianic congregation, Beth Yeshua, wants to be a bridge between Messianic Jews and non-Jewish believers who love Israel.

The choice of a meeting place could not have been better. It is an eighteenth-century house beside one of the beautiful canals in downtown Amsterdam. A stone's throw from there, the statue 'De Dokwerker' is a reminder of the 'February Strike' during World War II. An all-out strike was called when the population of Amsterdam discovered that trains full of Jews were being sent to extermination camps in Germany. The world-famous Portuguese Synagogue is not far from there either.

Even the beautiful eighteenth-century houses along the canals have something to do with the promise, 'I will bless you if you bless my people.' When, in the last century, Jews were expelled from Spain and other South European countries, many fled to the North and found a 'Mokum', a good place, in Amsterdam ('Mokum' is a common Dutch name for Amsterdam), which resulted in the Golden Age, with the increase in trade and art. God's blessing came to our land after we blessed the Jews.

The Beth Yeshua meeting was a mixture of social contact, including coffee and cake, celebration with songs of praise and worship, and an address. Everything was translated into English for a group of Russian Jews. They represented the problems of modern times: the collapse of the Soviet Union and the fear of rising anti-Semitism. But also of the fulfilment of God's certain promise, 'I will bring you back from the countries in the north.'

Leon asked me to give an eye-witness account of what God is doing among the Jews. I chose as a text Matthew 24:32, the promise of the 'blossoming of the fig tree'. Jesus showed that a sign of the coming again of the Messiah is the physical and spiritual restoration of Israel.

When I looked around, I tried to realise what this meeting signified: a fresh, new, vital group of Messianic Jews united with Christians. That is the way in which the Lord will work in the end times, restoring Israel and breaking down the dividing wall. How promising! Just as at the beginning of my adventure in Jerusalem, so now I again felt I was part of something bigger than I could possibly understand.

The end times are upon us. Years of great tribulation lie before us. Great disturbances in nature, earthquakes, floods and droughts will come. Political instability will increase, so that nation will stand up against nation, people against people. Just as in childbirth, the pains will increase until the birth of the new kingdom is completed.

But in the meantime, the ingathering of God's people as

a great, ripe harvest will continue. More and more Jews will find the Messiah, some by revelation, some by reading the New Testament and some by the testimony of another believer, Jew or Gentile. God's Spirit will breathe over the earth and quicken new spiritual life, revelation and restoration. The veil will be lifted, and as a result, Jews will see that Yeshua is the promised one.

I saw the beginning of this process and stood in awe. The dry bones of Ezekiel's vision are moving and will come to life through the wind of the Spirit.

Messianic Prophecies

There are many types in the Old Testament with a prophetic similitude to the coming Messiah, Jesus. For example, Isaac, the son of the patriarch Abraham, was almost sacrificed. According to Hebrews 11:17–19 this created faith in a resurrection. Consider the life of Joseph: his brothers tried to kill him, but finally it was he who saved them from dying of hunger, even though they didn't realise who he was at first. And so there are many types of Jesus to be found in the *Tenach*.

Old Testament:
Psalm 35:19; 38:19: Hate without reason.
New Testament:
John 15:25: They hated me without reason.

Old Testament:
Psalm 69:21: They put gall in my food and gave me vinegar for my thirst.
New Testament:
Matthew 27:48; Mark 15:36; Luke 23:36; John 19:29: One

man ran, filled a sponge with wine vinegar, put it on a stick, and offered it to Jesus to drink.

Old Testament:
Psalm 69:25 about the adversaries of the anointed: May their place be deserted.

New Testament:
Acts 1:19–20 about Judas: So they called that field in their language Akeldama, that is, Field of Blood. For . . . it is written in the Book of Psalms: may his place be deserted, let there be no one to dwell in it.

Old Testament:
Psalm 22:1: My God, my God, why have you forsaken me?

New Testament:
Matthew 27:46: About the ninth hour Jesus cried out in a loud voice, *'Eloi, Eloi, lama sabachthani?'*—which means, 'My God, my God, why have you forsaken me?'

Old Testament:
Psalm 22:18: They divide my garments among them and cast lots for my clothing.

New Testament:
John 19:23–24: When the soldiers crucified Jesus, they took his clothes, dividing them into four shares, one for each of them, with the undergarment. . . . 'Let's not tear it,' they said to one another. 'Let's decide by lot who will get it.' This happened that the Scripture might be fulfilled which said, 'They divided my garments among them and cast lots for my clothing.'

Old Testament:
Psalm 91:11–12: For he will command his angels concerning you to guard you in all your ways; they will lift you up in their hands, so that you will not strike your foot against a stone.

New Testament:
Matthew 4:6; Luke 4:9–11: The devil led him to Jerusalem and had him stand on the highest point of the temple. 'If you are the Son of God,' he said, 'throw yourself down from here. For it is written: "He will command his angels concerning you to guard you carefully; they will lift you up in their hands, so that you will not strike your foot against a stone."'

Old Testament:
Psalm 95:7–11: Today, if you hear his voice, do not harden your hearts as you did at Meribah.
New Testament:
Hebrews 3:7–11; 4:7: Today, if you hear his voice do not harden your hearts.

Old Testament:
Psalm 97:7: Worship him, all you gods!
New Testament:
Hebrews 1:6: Let all God's angels worship him.

Old Testament:
Psalm 102:25–27: In the beginning you laid the foundations of the earth, and the heavens are the work of your hands . . . but you remain the same.
New Testament:
Hebrews 1:8–10: But about the Son. . . . In the beginning O Lord, you laid the foundations of the earth, and the heavens are the work of your hands.

Old Testament:
Psalm 110:1: The Lord says to my Lord: 'Sit at my right hand until I make your enemies a footstool for your feet.'
New Testament:
Matthew 22:44; Mark 12:36; Luke 20:42–43; Acts 2:34–35; 1 Corinthians 15:25; Hebrews 1:13: The Lord said to my Lord: 'Sit at my right hand until I put your enemies under your feet.'

Old Testament:

Psalm 110:4: The Lord has sworn and will not change his mind: 'You are a priest for ever, in the order of Melchizedek.'

New Testament:

Hebrews 5:5–7: So Christ also did not take upon himself the glory of becoming a high priest. But God said to him, 'You are my Son; today I have become your Father.' . . . 'You are a priest for ever, in the order of Melchizedek.'

Old Testament:

Psalm 118:22: The stone the builders rejected has become the capstone.

New Testament:

Matthew 21:42; Mark 12:10–11; Luke 20:17; 1 Peter 2:7: Haven't you read this scripture: 'The stone the builders rejected has become the capstone; the Lord has done this, and it is marvellous in our eyes'?

Acts 4:10–12: It is by the name of Jesus Christ of Nazareth, whom you crucified but whom God raised from the dead, that this man stands before you completely healed. He is 'the stone you builders rejected, which has become the capstone'. Salvation is found in no one else, for there is no other name under heaven given to men by which we must be saved.

Old Testament:

Psalm 118:26: Blessed is he who comes in the name of the Lord.

New Testament:

Matthew 21:9; 23:39; Mark 11:9; Luke 13:35; John 12:13: The crowds that went ahead of him and those that followed shouted, 'Hosanna to the Son of David!' 'Blessed is he who comes in the name of the Lord!' 'Hosanna in the highest!'

Old Testament:
2 Samuel 7:16; Psalm 132:11: The Lord swore . . . to David
. . . 'One of your own descendants I will place on your
throne. . . .'

New Testament:
Luke 1:69–70; Acts 2:30; 13:22–23: He made David their
king. He testified concerning him: 'I have found David son
of Jesse a man after my own heart . . .' From this man's
descendants God has brought to Israel the Saviour Jesus, as
he promised.

Old Testament:
Isaiah 7:14: The virgin will be with child and will give birth
to a son, and will call him Immanuel.

New Testament:
Matthew 1:22–23: All this took place to fulfil what the Lord
had said through the prophet: The virgin will be with child
and will give birth to a son, and they will call him
Immanuel—which means, God with us.

Old Testament:
Isaiah 9:2: The people walking in darkness have seen a great
light; on those living in the land of the shadow of death a
light has dawned.

New Testament:
Matthew 4:13–16: Leaving Nazareth, he went and lived in
Capernaum . . . to fulfil what was said through the prophet
Isaiah. . . . The people living in darkness have seen a great
light.

Old Testament:
Genesis 3:15: Enmity between you and the woman, and
between your offspring and hers; he will crush your
head.

New Testament:
Galatians 4:4: But when the time had fully come, God sent
his Son, born of a woman, born under law, to redeem those
under law, that we might receive the full rights of sons.

Old Testament:
Genesis 12:3: And all peoples on earth will be blessed through you.
New Testament:
Matthew 1:1; Acts 3:25: A record of the genealogy of Jesus Christ the son of David, the son of Abraham.
Galatians 3:16: The promises were spoken to Abraham and to his seed. The Scripture does not say 'and to seeds', meaning many people, but 'and to your seed', meaning one person, who is Christ.

Old Testament:
Psalm 2:7; Proverbs 30:4: He said to me, 'You are my Son; today I have become your Father.'
New Testament:
Matthew 3:17; Luke 1:32–33: He will be great and will be called the Son of the Most High. The Lord God will give him the throne of his father David, and he will reign over the house of Jacob for ever; his kingdom will never end.

Old Testament:
Micah 5:2: But you, Bethlehem Ephrathah . . . out of you will come for me one who will be ruler over Israel, whose origins are from of old, from ancient times.
New Testament:
Matthew 2:1; Luke 2:4–7: So Joseph also went up from the town of Nazareth in Galilee to Judea, to Bethlehem the town of David, because he belonged to the house and line of David.

Old Testament:
Isaiah 61:1: The Spirit of the Sovereign Lord is on me, because the Lord has anointed me to preach good news to the poor. He has sent me to bind up the broken-hearted.
New Testament:
Luke 4:16–21: He went to Nazareth, where he had been brought up, and on the Sabbath day he went into the

synagogue, as was his custom. And he stood up to read.
The scroll of the prophet Isaiah was handed to him.
Unrolling it, he found the place where it is written: The
Spirit of the Lord is on me . . . then he rolled up the scroll,
gave it back to the attendant and sat down . . . and he began
by saying to them, 'Today this scripture is fulfilled in your
hearing.'

Old Testament:
Isaiah 35:4–6; 42:18: He will come to save you. Then will
the eyes of the blind be opened and the ears of the deaf
unstopped. Then will the lame leap like a deer, and the
tongue of the dumb shout for joy.
New Testament:
Matthew 11:4–6: Jesus replied, 'Go back and report to John
what you hear and see: The blind receive sight, the lame
walk, those who have leprosy are cured, the deaf hear, the
dead are raised, and the good news is preached to the poor.'

Old Testament:
Isaiah 53:9: Though he had done no violence, nor was any
deceit in his mouth.
New Testament:
1 Peter 2:21–23: Because Christ suffered for you, leaving
you an example. . . . He committed no sin, and no deceit
was found in his mouth. When they hurled their insults at
him, he did not retaliate, when he suffered, he made no
threats.

Old Testament:
Zechariah 9:9: Shout, daughter of Jerusalem! See, your king
comes to you, righteous and having salvation, gentle and
riding on a donkey.
New Testament:
Matthew 21:1–11; Mark 11:1–11: When they brought the
colt to Jesus and threw their cloaks over it, he sat on it. . . .
Those who went ahead and those who followed shouted,

'Hosanna!' 'Blessed is he who comes in the name of the Lord!' 'Blessed is the coming kingdom of our father David!' 'Hosanna in the highest!'

Old Testament:

Isaiah 53:9: He was assigned a grave with the wicked, and with the rich in his death.

New Testament:

Matthew 27:57–60: As evening approached, there came a rich man from Arimathea, named Joseph. . . . Joseph took the body, wrapped it in a clean linen cloth, and placed it in his own new tomb.

Old Testament:

Psalm 16:10: Because you will not abandon me to the grave, nor will you let your Holy One see decay.

New Testament:

Matthew 28:1–20; Acts 2:24–36; 13:33–37: But God raised him from the dead, freeing him from the agony of death. . . . David said about him: 'I saw the Lord always before me. Because he is at my right hand, I will not be shaken.'

Glossary

Agnosticism—term first used by T.H. Huxley to denote the theory that we know nothing of things beyond material phenomena.

Aliyah—literally, to go up. To be called to take the place next to the one who reads aloud in the *shul*. This is considered an honour. Also, emigration to Israel.

Bar Mitzvah—literally, son of the commandment. At thirteen years of age a Jewish boy becomes an adult as far as religious matters are concerned. He has to read a piece from the *Torah*, with the blessings that go with it. For girls, *Bat Mitzvah* is celebrated at twelve years of age.

Blessing and cursing—the mountains Gerizim and Ebal in the region of Sheichem symbolise the blessings and the curses which are mentioned in the *Torah*.

Challot—sabbath bread.

Chanukah—in 168 BC the aging priest Mattathias and his five sons rebelled against the attempt by the Seleucid king Antiochus IV to transform Jerusalem into a Greek city and root out the Jewish religion altogether. This had culminated in Antiochus placing a statue of Zeus in the Temple and sacrificing pigs on the altar. The struggle was continued by his son Judas Maccabeus. Victory was eventually gained and the Temple was reconsecrated. A miracle happened in that a bottle containing just enough oil for one day kept the menorah burning in the Temple for eight days. That is why in commemoration an eight-armed candlestick is lit, a light for every day.

Chassidism—movement within Judaism founded by Israel Ba'al Shem Tow from the Ukraine, emphasising piety and prayer. God is also served in joy, dancing and singing. Their motto is Psalm 100:2, 'Serve the Lord with gladness.'

Cheder—school where children from the age of three learn Hebrew and are taught the *Torah* and *Talmud*.

Chet—sin.

Diaspora—the dispersion of the Jews outside Israel.

Displaced persons—refugees.

Eretz Israel—the land of Israel. Actually, only in the land of Israel is Judaism fully expressed, because some of the 613 commandments and prohibitions apply only to Israel.

Since the destruction of the Second Temple, Jews have prayed daily for a return to their country and the restoration of the Temple. While praying, people face in the direction of Jerusalem three times a day. Should a Jew be buried in the *diaspora*, a few grains of earth from Israel are buried with him as a symbol of his unity with Eretz Israel.

Erev Shabbat—evening before the Sabbath, Friday evening. The table, laid with a white tablecloth, forms an altar, on which arc placed the *challot*, the lighted candles and the *kiddush* wine, increasing the sense of sanctity.

Etrog—citrus fruit which is used, together with the *lulav*, during the Feast of Tabernacles.

Gefilte fish—typical Jewish dish made of carp filled, among other things, with potatoes and carrots.

Genealogy—a family tree.

G'eulah Sh'lemah—the complete redemption of Israel.

Goy—Gentile.

Haftarah—literally, conclusion. On the Sabbath, after the reading from the law, and a passage from the prophets, the *Haftarah* is said.

Haggadah—literally, narration. Liturgy for *Pesach*. A book in which the story of the Exodus from Egypt is told.

Halachah—Jewish conduct in life. Literally, the going. The Jewish normative laws from the *Torah* as well as the *Talmud*.

Holocaust—Greek for 'burnt offering'. Destruction of the Jews during World War II.

Karma—Hindu and Buddhist dogma which says that the quality of our actions—good and bad—determine our future destiny.

Kehilat Brit—literally, community of the covenant.

Kibbutz—community of pioneers who have no private possessions and no hierarchy, who set up a communal settlement and devote themselves to working on the land. Plural—kibbutzim.

Kiddush—sanctification. Blessing spoken over a cup of wine at the beginning of the Sabbath.

Kippah—head covering for men.

Kosher—fulfilling the requirements of the Jewish food laws, based on Leviticus 11 and Deuteronomy 14. Maintains among other things a strict separation between milk and meat dishes.

L'shanah haba'ah b'irushalayim—'next year in Jerusalem'. This hope has been voiced aloud at the end of the *Pesach* celebration by Jews in the *diaspora* for 2,000 years.

Lithuanian tradition—the great rabbis in the last 200 years have come from Lithuania. This tradition places the emphasis on the law, with a strong desire for an increase in theoretical knowledge. Opposed to Chassidism.

Lulav—palm, myrtle and willow branches bound together
and used during *Succoth* (Feast of Tabernacles).

Mikvah—ritual bath in which people immerse themselves
totally. Women use it before the marriage ceremony
and after menstruation.

Moshav—co-operative agricultural community with greater
independence than in a kibbutz.

Moshava—agricultural village which is not a co-operative.

Netivyah—way of the Lord.

Pesach—the celebration of the liberation from slavery in
Egypt and, with that, the birth of the Jewish nation.
The word itself means 'passed over', because the angel
of death who killed the firstborn of the Egyptians
passed over the Jews who had put blood on their door
posts.

Replacement theology—teaching which says that the church
replaces Israel.

Rosh Hashanah—Jewish New Year. Part of a series of
celebrations inviting repentance.

Ruach Hakodesh—the Holy Spirit.

Sabra—born Israelite. A fruit of the cactus, prickly on the
outside, soft on the inside.

Seder—Passover table with symbolic foods enjoyed during
the two evenings before *Pesach*. During this time stories
are told about the journey out of Egypt.

Shabbat—day of rest between sunset on Friday evening and
sunset on Saturday evening, devoted to studying the
Torah, prayer and rest in order to come to repentance.

Sharav—hot, dry desert wind.

Sha'ul—Hebrew name for Paul.

Shavuoth—weeks, or Pentecost. In remembrance of the
giving of the law on Mount Sinai. An agricultural feast
at the start of the summer harvest.

Shema Yisrael, Adonai Elohenu, Adonai Echad—'Hear, O
Israel: The Lord our God, the Lord is one.' The most
important Jewish profession of faith, found in Deuteronomy 6:4.

Shul—synagogue, house of meeting.

Siddur—book of daily prayers. Also contains short prayers for different feasts and fasts.

Simchat Torah—the Joy of the Law. The reading of the *Torah* is completed after a year and begins again with Genesis. The *Torah* scrolls are carried around the *shul*, accompanied by dancing and rejoicing.

Succah—booth.

Talmud—Encyclopedia of Jewish learning. The product of the cultural life of the Jewish people from the Babylonian exile to approximately AD 600. Comprising the *Mishna* (repetition) and *Gemara* (completion), in which the rabbis comment on the *Torah* and explain how God's law is to be applied in practice.

Tashlich—custom in which people on *Rosh Hashanah*, the Jewish New Year, refer to Micah 7:18–20, where it says that God throws our sins into the depths of the sea. People walk along a stretch of running water and shake out crumbs from their pockets.

Tenach—Old Testament. Consists of its *Torah* (books of Moses), *Neviim* (prophets), and *Ketuvim* (writings).

Torah—the five books of Moses (Genesis to Deuteronomy).

Ulpan—language school.

Wadi—dry river bed.

Yeshiva—college for Talmudic study, which leads to rabbinical qualifications. The most important *Yeshivot* are in Jerusalem and in Ben Berak near Tel Aviv.

Yeshua HaMashiach—Jesus the Messiah.

Yom Kippur—Day of Atonement, with the most important purpose being penance, caused by a sincere desire to recognise and acknowledge sins and a willingness to turn back from the wrong path. From sunset until the following evening there is fasting.

Appointment in Jerusalem

by Lydia Prince
as told to her husband Derek Prince

The true story of a schoolteacher who dared to be led by the
Holy Spirit . . . and of the city where God has hidden the key to
the future.

Lydia had everything. Education, money, social position . . . a
fulfilling professional life as head of a department at her school
. . . a luxurious apartment with a devoted maid to care for it . . .
parties, dancing, admiring friends, expensive clothes . . . and a
proposal of marriage. What strange series of events led her to
abandon all this and journey alone and penniless to an alien
land where she would experience almost daily danger?

Appointment in Jerusalem is the unforgettable true story of a
twentieth century woman who dared to take the Bible at its
literal face value and in so doing discovered what many seek
but few ever find. Joy. Peace. Perfect security — no matter how
desperate the external condition of her life.

Lydia Prince resided for twenty years in Jerusalem where she
mothered scores of abandoned Jewish and Arab children and
witnessed the birth of modern Israel. At the close of World War
II, she married Derek Prince and the couple had nine adopted
daughters from Jewish, Arab, British and African backgrounds.

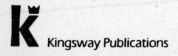

Kingsway Publications

Battle for Israel

by Lance Lambert

Israel — not just for the tourist.
It's a geographical knot in a tug of war between the
super powers.

This book takes you into the political as well as
the spiritual conflict.
Written by a man with inside information.
He presents a perspective not to be found
anywhere else.

Lance Lambert, long time friend of prominent
Israeli leaders and an authority on the Bible history
of the Israeli nation, is the author. He gives an 'on
the scene' account of the Yom Kippur War — he
predicts the future — his insight is unique.

Never before has one man been allowed to enter
into the confidence of Israelis to such an extent —
Lambert, a Christian, welcomed and loved by
Jews, describes the Battle for Israel.

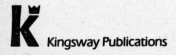

Kingsway Publications

The Uniqueness Of Israel

by Lance Lambert

Woven into the fabric of Jewish existence there is an undeniable uniqueness. Israel's terrain, her history and chief city, all owe their uniqueness to the fact that God's appointed Saviour for the world was born a Jew. His destiny and theirs are for ever intertwined.

There is bitter controversy over the subject of Israel, but time itself will establish the truth about this nation's place in God's plan. For Lance Lambert, the Lord Jesus is the key that unlocks Jewish history. He is the key not only to their fall, but also to their restoration. For in spite of the fact that they rejected him, he has not rejected them.

K

Kingsway Publications

Blood Brothers

by **Elias Chacour** *with David Hazard*

'The Jews and Palestinians are brothers, blood brothers,' said
father. 'We share the same father—Abraham—and the same
God. We must never forget that.'

Despite his father's words of peace, Elias Chacour sensed even
as a child that enmity and mistrust were not so easily overcome.

Once Christian and Jew had shared the simple things of life
together. But 1948 changed all that. The Zionists came, and
almost a million Palestinians were made homeless. An exile in
his own land, Elias faced the horrors of violence when tens of
thousands lost their lives.

Then his father, his brother, and most of the village men
disappeared.

In the years that followed, Elias struggled to find a way of peace
that would avoid violence and yet accomplish more than his
father's passive attitude. Then, just as he was about to begin a
quiet life of service to the church, he received a new and
dangerous calling that would take him right through the
world's most bitter conflict.

A way of hope and reconciliation beckoned.

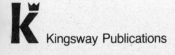
Kingsway Publications